Visualising Literacy and How to Teach It

Technological advances and the way young people interact with them means children are thinking and processing information in an increasingly visual manner. *Visualising Literacy and How to Teach It* recognises that many, if not most, children are attracted to visual images and uses this as a basis for introducing and developing a range of thinking skills and strategies for learning. This practical resource offers a selection of visuals, each accompanied by activities that give children practice in using their imaginations in different ways.

Visualising Literacy and How to Teach It not only explores creative and critical thinking skills but also pays close attention to the overarching thinking skill that we call imagination. The book contains around 150 practical activities that develop children's imaginations, focussing on a range of thinking skills, including but not limited to the following:

- developing observational/attentional skills
- noticing details (focussing of attention)
- assimilating visual information
- increasing experience of inferential thinking, speculation, dealing with generalisations
- boosting vocabulary
- empowering one's attitude towards exploring ideas
- learning different questioning techniques
- increasing the ability to empathise
- becoming comfortable with uncertainty and ambiguity

Many of the visualisation techniques can be applied to developing different aspects of emotional resourcefulness, including empathy, positive self-image, anchoring positive thoughts and modifying negative thoughts and feelings. This is, therefore, an essential resource for any teacher or education professional who is keen on developing children's ability to think and express their own ideas.

Steve Bowkett taught secondary English for 20 years before becoming a full-time author. He has written fiction for adults and children of all ages, plus educational books on literacy, thinking skills, creativity, philosophy and emotional resourcefulness.

Tony Hitchman has over 35 years of experience teaching throughout the primary age range in diverse schools culminating in 11 years as a primary headteacher. He has frequently collaborated with Steve Bowkett on books and projects to develop children's literacy and creativity.

Visualising Literacy and How to Teach It

A Guide to Developing Thinking Skills, Vocabulary and Imagination for 9–12 Year Olds

Steve Bowkett and Tony Hitchman

LONDON AND NEW YORK

First published 2022
by Routledge
2 Park Square, Milton Park, Abingdon, Oxon OX14 4RN

and by Routledge
605 Third Avenue, New York, NY 10158

Routledge is an imprint of the Taylor & Francis Group, an informa business

© 2022 Steve Bowkett and Tony Hitchman

The right of Steve Bowkett and Tony Hitchman to be identified as authors of this work has been asserted by them in accordance with sections 77 and 78 of the Copyright, Designs and Patents Act 1988.

All rights reserved. The purchase of this copyright material confers the right on the purchasing institution to photocopy pages which bear the photocopy icon and copyright line at the bottom of the page. No other parts of this book may be reprinted or reproduced or utilised in any form or by any electronic, mechanical, or other means, now known or hereafter invented, including photocopying and recording, or in any information storage or retrieval system, without permission in writing from the publishers.

Trademark notice: Product or corporate names may be trademarks or registered trademarks, and are used only for identification and explanation without intent to infringe.

British Library Cataloguing-in-Publication Data
A catalogue record for this book is available from the British Library

Library of Congress Cataloging-in-Publication Data
Names: Bowkett, Stephen, author. | Hitchman, Tony, 1952 author.
Title: Visualising literacy and how to teach it : using images and visualisation techniques to develop children's thinking skills, imagination, vocabulary and emotional resourcefulness for 9-12 year olds / Steve Bowkett and Tony Hitchman.
Description: Abingdon, Oxon ; New York, NY : Routledge, 2022. | Includes bibliographical references and index. | Identifiers: LCCN 2021014081 | ISBN 9781032025773 (hardback) | ISBN 9781032025797 (paperback) | ISBN 9781003184003 (ebook)
Subjects: LCSH: Visual literacy. | Thought and thinking—Study and teaching (Elementary) | Imagination in children. | Emotions in children.
Classification: LCC LB1068 .B68 2022 | DDC 370.1523—dc23
LC record available at https://lccn.loc.gov/2021014081

ISBN: 978-1-032-02577-3 (hbk)
ISBN: 978-1-032-02579-7 (pbk)
ISBN: 978-1-003-18400-3 (ebk)

DOI: 10.4324/9781003184003

Typeset in Bembo and Helvetica Neue LT Pro
by Apex CoVantage, LLC

Steve – To Wendy as always with love.

Tony – To Sue – as always.

In memory of our friend Mark Taylor (Marcula) – Requiescet in pace.

Thanks to paleoanthropologist Genevieve von Petzinger for permission to reproduce Figure 40.5 from her book *The First Signs*.

Contents

List of figures   x

1. Using this book and introduction   1
2. Some definitions   3
3. Educational benefits of developing imagination   5
4. The attitude   7
5. Mind warmups   9
6. Picture exploration – a medley of thinking skills   11
7. Questioning with confidence   20
8. Collecting motifs   22
9. Colour combinations   26
10. Subtle distinctions   29
11. Sound work   35
12. Submodalities   40
13. Step in – the physical dimension   41

14	What's the feeling?	44
15	Two anecdotes	46
16	Just enough	48
17	Sensory treasures	51
18	Spelling strategies	53
19	Break state	55
20	Minimal writing and artful vagueness	57
21	Cross-matching senses	62
22	Drawing out meaning	65
23	Point of view	67
24	Picture masking	70
25	Beyond the frame	72
26	Cinematic method of describing a picture	75
27	Studying pictures	77
28	Sensory journey	78
29	Educational value of the sensory journey	81
30	Vivid particularities	83
31	Creative conversations	86
32	Imagining impossible things	91
33	More thought experiments	93
34	Inspiration	98
35	A medley of visualisations	100

36	Reframing	103
37	Scrambletales	106
38	Linking game	110
39	Descriptive writing	112
40	Some literary devices for descriptive writing	117
41	Pictograms and hieroglyphs	125
42	Letter associations	130
43	Describing phonemes	131
44	Interpreting abstract shapes	133
45	Venn diagrams	138
46	'Sliderman'	141
47	Heads or tails	143
48	Dice journey	150
49	Controlling the imagination	155
50	Tackling text	157
51	Thoughts, feelings, memories and dreams	160
52	Mindfulness	161
53	A special place	163
54	Imagination beyond the curriculum	172

References and resources   *173*
Index   *177*

Figures

6.1	Cat on the corner 1	12
6.2	Why is this man smiling 1	14
6.3	Why is this man smiling 2	14
6.4	Why is this man smiling 3	15
6.5	Maybe hand	17
7.1	Heavy seas	20
8.1	Space romance	23
8.2	Knocking on the door	24
8.3	Hut on the cliff	24
9.1	Cat on the corner 2	26
14.1	The Lonely Forest	44
16.1	Exploring the crypt	49
20.1	Deleted dialogue	59
21.1	Emotions and landscape features	63
21.2	Abstract shapes for character exploration	64
24.1	What's going on here 1	70
24.2	What's going on here 2	71
24.3	What's going on here 3	71
25.1	Cat on the corner 3	73
26.1	Weary rider	76
35.1	Storyline	100
36.1	All will be revealed	104
37.1	Scrambletales	107
37.2	Ralph saves Bertha	108
38.1	Linking game	111
39.1	Word cloud – colour association white	115
40.1	Connotations 1	119
40.2	Connotations 2	120
40.3	Funfair	121
40.4	Abstract shapes	122
40.5	Symbols	123
40.6	Rock art symbols	124
41.1	Evolution of K	125
41.2	Hieroglyphs	126

41.3	Cartouches of Steve and Tony	127
41.4	Love and Justice	128
41.5	Demon, cupid, warrior and praying figure	129
44.1	Character traits 1	134
44.2	Character traits 2	134
44.3	Character traits 3	135
44.4	Abstract emotions	136
44.5	Abstract anger	136
45.1	Overlapping circles	139
46.1	Sliderman	142
48.1	Compass points	151
48.2	Dice journey	152

CHAPTER

Using this book and introduction

All of the activities in *Visualising Literacy and How to Teach It* aim to help children to use their imaginations more effectively. A number of associated thinking skills are covered through dozens of practical how-to techniques. We have sequenced these loosely throughout the book, though you may prefer to cherry-pick particular activities to fit in with your own programmes of study. Because of this we have repeated certain principles and ideas a number of times: these serve as rationales for using the techniques and strengthen their educational underpinning. We have also cross-referenced activities to make creating sequenced programmes easier. While we emphasise creative writing and emotional resourcefulness in the book, we also show how the thinking skills and use of the imagination are useful (one might argue necessary) in areas such as science, history, philosophy and others. You will also find that on occasions, we suggest the exact words you can use when instructing children to carry out the task: we're not trying to be deliberately didactic, but often the particular way in which an activity is framed has a powerful influence on how children respond.

Albert Einstein famously said that imagination is more important than knowledge. He also maintained that imagination rather than knowledge was the true sign of intelligence. Most simply put, imagination is the ability we have to form and control images in the mind: the word 'idea' derives from the Greek meaning picture, form and pattern (though as we'll see, it's about more than just images). And while the definition of intelligence is complex and to some extent controversial, we can agree perhaps that intelligent thinking manipulates knowledge rather than just stores and recalls it. This also implies the creative use of knowledge, insofar as it links previously separate ideas to generate new insights and deepen understanding, bearing in mind that to have knowledge of something is not necessarily to understand it. As such, imaginative manipulation of knowledge generates information, which can be read as 'in-formation'; the formation of clearer meanings[1] and greater comprehension. This in turn leads to what is commonly called the inner world of the mind, which powerfully shapes our perceptions of the world 'out there'. The inner world is also no less interesting and open for exploration than the outside world – together constituting what we can call the 'real' world we live in.

Note

1. Professor Kieran Egan (cited in the following chapter) highlights the importance of 'meaning making' as a key aspect of true education. Similarly, educationalist Neil Postman and writer Charles Weingartner (Postman and Weingartner (1971)) quote the philosopher and communications guru Marshall McLuhan, who asserts that humans are 'meaning making machines'. To facilitate this ability, Postman and Weingartner advocated the enquiry method of education, where learning is focussed on students asking questions rather than just being fed facts.

CHAPTER

Some definitions

Definitions of imagination vary. Educationalist Kieran Egan explores the topic in detail (Egan (2002)), pointing out that the main Hebrew term for imagination is 'yetser', whose root is the same as 'yetsirah', which translates as 'creation'. That in turn prompts the question of what creativity is and whether it amounts to the same thing as imagination.

Since this is intended to be a practical resource book to develop children's thinking, we offer what are some hopefully pragmatic definitions around the idea of imagination.

- Creativity. The act of bringing something new into existence. In terms of thinking, a creative idea is one formed when two or more previously unconnected thoughts are brought together. Etymologically, the word comes from Latin meaning to produce, bring forth, grow and is linked to Ceres, the Roman goddess of agriculture. (In this context, note the agricultural metaphors for learning on page 10.)
- Daydreaming. To daydream is to be more or less aware of the thoughts streaming through the mind. We can make a distinction between 'idle daydreaming' when we might hardly notice those thoughts, being 'lost in reverie', and 'systematic/ deliberate daydreaming' when we guide and prompt thoughts with a clear purpose or intention in mind. Most of the activities in this book aim to promote deliberate daydreaming, which is one aspect of metacognition: the ability to notice and manipulate one's thoughts.
- Idea. Can we get away with saying an idea is a 'unit of thought', which we may receive passively from elsewhere and do nothing with it or creatively and imaginatively put it together with other ideas to produce something new? The word itself comes from the Greek 'to see' and 'form, pattern', which leans more towards the active manipulation of mental content.
- Imagination. Again coming from Latin and meaning to 'picture to oneself'. But as we've already suggested, imagination goes beyond just thinking

visually. Egan in *Imagination in Teaching and Learning* (Egan (2002)) asserts that the imagination is a kind of meeting point where perception, memory, ideas, metaphor, emotion and a range of other kinds of thinking work together. As hinted previously, imagination is an elusive concept, though we can usually recognise an imaginative idea when it appears.

- Originality. Robin Barrow (1990) suggests that an imaginative idea is one that is unusual and effective. This touches on the notion of originality. If creativity involves bringing ideas together in a new way, then as children's creativity and imaginations develop, they will have more ideas that are original *to them* – ideas that they have not thought about before, even if in the general scheme of things those ideas are well-known. True originality in the form of completely new ideas represents imagination elevated to a very high degree. In our opinion this has profound implications for what learning means, going beyond the simple delivery of 'facts' and their subsequent recall under test conditions. True education must require children to actively do something more with the information they are given. This goes to the heart of information as 'in-formation', the creation of fresh insights and deeper understanding.

If we allow this take on originality then we can acknowledge two important principles in the development of children's thinking:

- To have our best ideas, we need to have lots of ideas.
- How many ideas can we have, and what use can we make of them?

Both principles recognise the generative power of the imagination. A creative person in whatever field will intend – and tend – to produce many ideas. Both principles also touch on the notion that generating ideas uses different modes of thinking than assessing or evaluating those ideas, once they have formed, to see if they are useful (or 'effective' to use Barrow's term). As such, while creative and critical thinking are not the same thing, they overlap and are mutually supportive. Simplistically, we can say that creative thinking produces the 'raw material' of lots of ideas that can then be reflected upon, analysed and evaluated to discover how well they fit their intended purpose.

Going beyond this, Egan (2002) argues that developing the imagination helps students to become more autonomous thinkers, able to see conventional ideas for what they are, presumably creating options to make use of more unconventional and original ideas. Clearly, to think unconventional thoughts in any area of enquiry, one needs to have an understanding of the conventions of that field. We look at this in the context of creative writing on page 68, though the notion has a much broader application.

As an aside to this, while many of the activities in the book are generic and can be applied across the subject range, we point out along the way how some can be used in topics found in science, geography, maths, physical education and mental/emotional resourcefulness.

CHAPTER 3

Educational benefits of developing imagination

The aim of this book is to use images and text to develop a range of thinking skills and strengthen the imagination, as it is in part defined in the previous chapter. We use the word 'strengthen' deliberately in line with the analogy that the imagination is like a muscle; the more it is exercised the stronger it becomes. We will also show how a strong imagination, coupled with an understanding of different ways of 'flexing' it, aids children's learning across the subject range and can also be beneficial in developing emotional resourcefulness and wellbeing: since the mind and body are linked, how we think as well as what we think influences how we feel and act.

We intend *Visualising Literacy* to be full of activities and techniques that can be used across a wide age and ability range. And because many of the activities prompt creative thinking, differentiation lies not so much in the materials themselves but in any child's response to them, given his or her current level of ability – i.e. differentiation by outcome. While some of the activities need to be run in a certain sequence as aspects of a wider visual exploration, others can be cherry-picked and used individually as 'mind warmups' or lesson starters to help prepare the children for further learning. We also discuss what we believe to be a useful attitude that you can cultivate in the children to help them get the most out of the picture-work that you do with them. Having said that, this book does not cover all aspects of visual literacy (for some excellent ideas along those lines, see, for instance, Browning Wroe and Lambert (2008); Stafford (2011) in 'References and Resources'). Rather, it is more broadly based and with an emphasis on how-to techniques for thinking rather than just helping children to 'read' images.

It is a cliché that a picture is worth a thousand words. Whether this is always true or not, certainly pictures can serve as springboards for *generating* words, thus encouraging children's language development and social interaction. As such, many of the activities can also be used for teaching languages other than a pupil's native tongue. Other educational benefits of working with pictures include the following:

Educational benefits

- developing observational/attentional skills
- noticing details (focussing of attention)
- boosting visualisation skills (together with understanding further applications of this)
- increasing concentration span
- assimilating visual information
- making creative connections
- increasing experience of inferential thinking, speculation, dealing with generalisations and other ways of thinking
- appreciating the mind-body link (your imagination goes right through you)
- developing metacognitive abilities across a range of sensory modes
- gaining experience of cross-matching sensory impressions to enrich ideas (synesthetic thinking)
- boosting vocabulary
- empowering one's attitude towards exploring ideas
- learning different questioning techniques
- increasing the ability to empathise
- becoming comfortable with uncertainty and ambiguity, etc.
- coupled with a reduced fear of the wrong answer, etc.
- coupled with a lessening need to know 'the right answer right now'
- becoming more familiar with criteria of relevance and quality in ideas and language

CHAPTER

The attitude

Children frequently ask us if they need to be clever to have ideas. Our answer is that they don't necessarily have to be clever, but they do need to be nosy. By this we mean noticing things and asking questions, these being the two core skills that underpin effective thinking. Younger children especially tend to be pleased and relieved to hear this because most already are nosy in these two important ways. For instance, Warren Berger in *A More Beautiful Question* notes that in a 2013 study it was found that the average four-year-old girl in the UK asks 390 questions a day, with boys of a similar age not far behind. (Berger (2014) page 4; see also the truthdive website. Numbers vary in other studies, it has to be said.) Perhaps this is linked to what, in some Eastern philosophical traditions, is called 'beginner's mind': looking at the world with fresh eyes and, as the educationist Margaret Meek says, with a sense of 'firstness', prompting the excitement and wonder that drive the questioning process.

As an aside, it would be interesting to find out how many questions older children ask, generally speaking. Granted, you could only do this in the classroom; and while we suspect that children ask fewer questions as the years go by, we'd be delighted to be proved wrong.

Noticing is a feature of mindfulness, which can also be termed 'present moment awareness'. Developing the ability to notice objects and one's own thoughts and feelings paves the way for the kind of attention (and appreciation) of things that characterise mindfulness. We look at this in more detail and note some of the benefits on page 161.

Being nosy by noticing and questioning similarly encourages creativity. Two important elements of this are

- making connections and
- looking at things in many different ways.

DOI: 10.4324/9781003184003-4

Any activity encouraging one or both of these behaviours has a creative underpinning. You can also help children to broaden and sharpen their range of thinking tools by

- making the thinking explicit.

In other words, feeding back to the children what they've done in their minds to respond to a task that you've given them. We explain how this works in the sequence of picture exploration activities next.

Once children have made a response, motivate them further by using

- quick feedback and
- sincere praise.

Quick feedback often simply means making the children's thinking explicit – i.e. letting them know what they've done. And because they *have* done some thinking for you, your praise is obviously sincere. Again, the picture exploration sequence of activities will show how these principles work in practice.

Finally, help the children to feel comfortable in thinking about and expressing their ideas by modelling the behaviour. In other words, tackle the activities yourself, along with the children, and let them know about your own ideas, confusions and difficulties too – being aware that in many cases there may be more than a single 'right answer' and maybe none at all, just a raft of possibilities and potential directions for taking the thinking further.

All of the aspects of what we've called 'the attitude' can be summed up by the acronym I-CAN – interested/individual, creative, active, nosy.

CHAPTER 5

Mind warmups

- Ask the children to look around the room. Point out to them that everything they notice began as an idea in someone's mind. That's an awful lot of good ideas just in one room! Also, ask the children if they understand the things they notice and if not to enquire about them. What's in a pencil so that it leaves a mark on paper? How is window glass made? How does a laptop work? Not knowing is at the outset just as good as knowing because it highlights the fact that not only do we as individuals live in a world filled with wonder and mystery but also there are so many things that we can *find out about*.
- Paying attention. As teachers perhaps we ask for this quite often, but like any other skill, it needs to be practised. Show the class an ordinary object such as an apple and instruct them to pay attention to it for two minutes.

After this time, ask for thoughts on what paying attention actually means. This can include children telling you what went on in their minds as they stared at the apple. Some children may have been fully focussed on the apple for the whole time. Others might have indulged in free association, where a thought that was linked to the apple began a chain of thinking that ended up somewhere else entirely. Yet others might have begun daydreaming almost at once, getting carried away in their thoughts and barely noticing that the apple was there at all; the visual equivalent of having a radio on somewhere nearby but hardly hearing the music or not hearing it at all. Also raise the issue of boredom. Which children got bored just staring at the apple? How would they define boredom? What can they do about it? (Read on!)

Children who kept their mental as well as their visual focus on the apple were, obviously, most closely paying attention as we usually use the term. You can help others to develop the skill by offering some prompts such as the following:

- Imagine picking up the apple. Feel the weight and texture.
- Imagine cutting the apple in half. Think about what the inside looks like.
- Imagine smelling the apple and then biting into it.

DOI: 10.4324/9781003184003-5

- Just noticing thoughts. Allowing thoughts to stream through the mind 'unhindered' is just as much a mental skill as paying attention. It's well-known that insights can suddenly appear – the aha! or eureka! moment – when the mind is otherwise idling.

Ask the children to think of a pleasant object or place. Some children will prefer to keep their eyes open for this, while others will want to close them. After perhaps 20 seconds tell the children to mentally relax: they can let the object or place fade away now. Then, as other thoughts begin to flow[1] through the mind, encourage children just to notice them going by without getting involved – i.e. without trying to manipulate the thoughts or get emotionally influenced by them. Append this by saying that if any unpleasant thoughts or memories do appear, children can simply open their eyes and/or deliberately think pleasant thoughts in their place. Another useful diversion is for the child to read a favourite book or comic or listen to some jokes.

Being able to stand back from one's thoughts is an ancient and powerful technique for increasing a sense of wellbeing. It's easy to get drawn into our memories or impressions of future experiences, and when these are not pleasant they are accompanied by negative emotions. Detaching from such thoughts limits the influence of the attendant unwanted feelings or prevents them from arising at all. An equally ancient technique to achieve this is to imagine thoughts as leaves drifting by in a stream, while we just observe them as we sit comfortably on the bank. They just come and go, come and go, as we just sit and watch.

This simple activity is a kind of meditation, a way of calming the mind and gently controlling our thoughts. For more, see, for example, Bowkett and Hogston (2017); Fontana and Slack (1997).

- Looking in. This activity combines the two previous activities.

Read a short extract from a story and ask children to notice what imagery and other impressions go through their minds as they listen. Noticing thoughts in this way is known as metacognition. Developing the skill will lead to a richer experience when children read or are read to but will also generate more details as they think about their writing. See also 'Creative Conversations' and 'Bare-Bones Writing' on pages 86 and 88.

Note

1. The water metaphor is useful in the context of thinking. We talk about thoughts streaming through the mind, stream-of-consciousness thinking, creative juices flowing, ideas drying up or (preferably) spraying or cascading into our awareness, images swirling around in the head, etc. As an extension of that, water can be combined with horticultural metaphors for learning: fertile soil, nourishing, strong roots, first shoots, flowering, the fruits of our endeavours, harvesting ideas and so on.

CHAPTER 6

Picture exploration – a medley of thinking skills

This activity underpins many of the others found throughout the book. It is modular, although you can take children through the whole process in one go if you wish. However, by showing them the picture a number of times, each time offering a different activity, you will establish a link in their minds between seeing the image and the positive feelings they experience as you show them various ways of thinking and the sincere praise you give them for doing so. This phenomenon is known as positive visual anchoring (page 114).

- Show the class the picture in Figure 6.1 and say, 'I'd like you to be nosy. Just notice anything at all in the picture and tell me what you've spotted'. In other words you're simply asking the children to notice and tell.

Because of the regime in many classrooms, where right answers tend to be rewarded, some children may be reticent to speak out in case they give a wrong answer: it's likely that the more confident children will have a go first. So a child might say, 'I've noticed the cat'. Your response can be, 'You spotted that cat, well done'. What you're doing here is giving quick feedback (you've done just what I asked you to do) and sincere praise because the child has self-evidently noticed something in the picture.

As other children join in all of the pupils come to realise that there is no hidden agenda behind the task. It is only a game of notice and tell. As such, less-confident children are likely to be tempted to take part since everyone enjoys sincere praise for having done something well. Some children might also wonder why you are asking them to do something so easy – but the point is that you are creating a learning environment whereby you can increase the intellectual/creative demands on the children while they continue to feel safe in their involvement with the activity.

Picture exploration

Figure 6.1 Cat on the corner 1

One 'danger point' comes if a child misidentifies something in the picture. This was flagged up for us when during one workshop a girl noticed the leaf at the bottom of the wall and said that someone had lost their slipper. Children sitting closer to the image chuckled and the girl blushed, feeling embarrassed. Our response was to let her look at a paper copy of the picture so that she could examine it more closely. She then said, 'Oh it's another leaf'.

The reply to give here is, 'Well done. You had the common sense to look again and the courage to change your mind'. This is a message that goes home to all of the children and is an example of what's called the principle of utilisation. This recognises that the children bring into the classroom whatever mental and emotional resources they possess at the time, at that stage of their learning, and that wherever possible as educators we aim to transform a negative experience into a positive one. What started out as something that might have knocked the girl's confidence was turned into a positive interaction that praised the child for her common sense and courage – qualities that earned her some sincere praise and which sent home the message to the rest of the class that these were valued traits in learning.

Although you initially asked the class to notice details in the picture and tell you about them, other kinds of thinking will happen as well: this is an ideal opportunity to make the children's thinking explicit; to feed back to them what they've done in responding to the task.

Before long a child is likely to say, 'Well I think it's been raining'. A useful reply is, 'You noticed that, well done. So what clues did you spot to give you that idea?' It's probable that the child noticed the puddles on the pavement, but you used the plural 'clues', which might prompt the child now to actively look for other details to support the idea. So the response might be, 'Well I saw the puddles, but look the sky's cloudy and the cat's fur is sticking out, maybe because it's damp'.

You – 'Good, so the puddles gave you the idea that it's been raining. But you also spotted the cloudy sky and the cat's fur, which might be sticking out because it's damp. Those other clues made your idea stronger and more likely. And I think that if there were even more clues in the picture, we could say it was more and more likely that it has recently been raining'.

This feeds back to all of the children the mental structure of inferential thinking, where an observation begins to form a hypothesis (a tentative explanation), which is strengthened by the addition of further observations acting as evidence. This kind of thinking is the basis of the scientific method of discovering more about the physical world. Once children begin to understand how inference works, one or more might come up with the idea that it's autumn because of the bare tree branches and the firework in the sky. (By the way, we call 'because' a sticky connective; whenever you use it you need to stick a reason onto it – 'I think it's autumn because of the bare branches and the firework in the sky'.)

- Speculation and interpretation.

If you run this activity, you might want to fit it in after the cat-on-the-corner workshop. We mention it here because it demonstrates to the children how speculation and interpretation are intertwined.

Show the class the image of the smiling man (Figure 6.2) and ask why he might be reacting like this. Because there is no evidence to support any reason the children's guesses will be pure speculation.

Follow up by showing the class the image in Figure 6.3. The children can now interpret the man's smile more accurately. The word 'interpret' incidentally comes from Latin and means to explain or translate.

Ask what feelings the man might be experiencing at that point – delight, pleasure, happiness, etc.

Now show the third image (Figure 6.4).

The children will have to interpret the smile differently (though some might still say the man is happy if he is getting rid of his arch-enemy).

- What other scenarios can the children think of that would attribute different emotions to the smiling man?
- Point out to the class how easy it can be to fall into the 'thinking trap' of jumping to conclusions. A more reasonable stance would be to hold back from making a decision in the absence of sufficient evidence. Sometimes we might never learn enough to make up our minds, in which case, ideally, we can feel

Picture exploration

Figure 6.2 Why is this man smiling 1

Figure 6.3 Why is this man smiling 2

Figure 6.4 Why is this man smiling 3

comfortable in the presence of ambiguity and uncertainty, tolerance of these being a valuable component of creative thinking in various fields of enquiry. The need to know 'the right answer right now' is often linked to the notion of success being predicated on knowing lots of right answers.

Highlighting interpretation and inferential thinking in this simple way prepares the ground for children to think like this but in a more sophisticated way in other subjects. In science and philosophy for example there is a kind of thinking called abduction – not kidnapping by aliens but 'inference to the best (most likely) explanation'. So using our cat picture, if we assume that the liquid on the pavement is water and given that the sky is cloudy and that the cat's fur is sticking out because it's damp, then we can be fairly sure that the most likely explanation is that it's been raining. Notice the if-then pattern of thinking (see page 18) and the fact that the idea is supported by three observations. Certainly, the nature of the liquid on the pavement could be tested, while the observation that the cloudy sky could well produce rain is consistent with past observations of cloudy skies producing rain. The dampness of the cat's fur is more open to speculation – the cat might have fallen in a pond or had a bucket of water thrown over it, or it might be angry or frightened. Ascertaining the reason could be difficult in that case.

In science the 'best' explanation usually means an idea or hypothesis that is based on observations and experiments, one that has the greatest explanatory power using the fewest assumptions (i.e. simplicity, see Occam's Razor on page 156) and one that can be falsified – that is, proved wrong in the light of further discoveries. Note though that sometimes what seems to be the correct explanation is not the simplest. In the case of atomic structure for example it used to be thought that the atom was composed simply of protons, neutrons and electrons: particle physics has since discovered that atoms are far more complex than this.

Prior to some children suggesting it's been raining, many may have commented on the light in the sky. Some think it's a firework, some think it's a comet and so on. A handy technique (literally) to use here is to get the children to hold out a hand, palm upwards. Tell them to pretend that the thing they've noticed is in the middle of the palm (the focus of attention). Then say, 'So maybe that light is a firework'. Fold your thumb inwards. 'Or maybe it's a comet'. Fold your index finger inwards. Then ask the class to come up with further maybe-ideas. Maybe it's a meteor, maybe it's a spaceship, maybe it's the fiery breath of a dragon, etc.

You have now demonstrated physically and visually the mental structure of speculation, where possible explanations radiate out from a central observation. Once you've collected five ideas – though you may get quite a few more – open out your fist and say, 'So look what we have now; a handful of ideas we can think about further'.

So the value of the maybe hand is as follows:

- It reinforces important principles mentioned earlier: making the thinking explicit, no hidden agenda, etc.
- It adds another thinking tool to the toolbox.
- It is a safe and inclusive activity. All the children can feel comfortable contributing (since the right answer, if there is one, is not known).
- It leads to more sophisticated ways of thinking and the discussion of ideas, such as the likelihood of explanations/supporting evidence/robust rationales behind hypotheses.
- Combined with other ways of thinking, it can be used across the curriculum thereby forming a strong and logistically effective cross-curricular link. So as well as making relevant connections between ideas in different subject domains at the level of themed content, use the thinking toolbox in different contexts.

So for instance you might decide to do a topic about water. The children can learn about the water cycle, the interesting properties of water, read a poem about water, pinpoint important rivers and lakes on a map, etc. But you can also set up lessons where the thinking skills they've already used can be practised.

- Why do cactus plants have spines rather than leaves?
- Why do leaves fall from deciduous trees in the autumn?
- Why aren't hailstones the same shape as snowflakes?
- What's the difference between mist and steam or fog and clouds?
- Does lightning ever happen in clear skies?
- Do fish drink?

What matters here is that when you put these kinds of questions to children (or when they ask them spontaneously), encourage them to use the ways of thinking they encounter in this book to *explore* ideas rather than get hung up immediately on 'right answers'. The great repository of knowledge that we as a species possess has been gathered not by having right answers handed to us on a plate but by often courageous people thinking about the world, sometimes in the face of fierce opposition through ignorance, bias, dogma, vested interests and overarching cultural paradigms.

Exploration like this builds towards what has been called the enquiry method of learning (see page 2). When children have a selection of possible explanations about some aspect of the topic they're studying, ask them how they might test or verify their ideas. Ask for reasoning and supporting evidence. This is also an opportunity to introduce or develop research skills, including looking at multiple sources, the relevance and recency of information, separating fact from opinion, looking at bias and hidden assumptions (see, for example, Langrehr (2008)/Rockett and Percival (2002)/Fogarty and Bellanca (2008) in 'References and Resources').

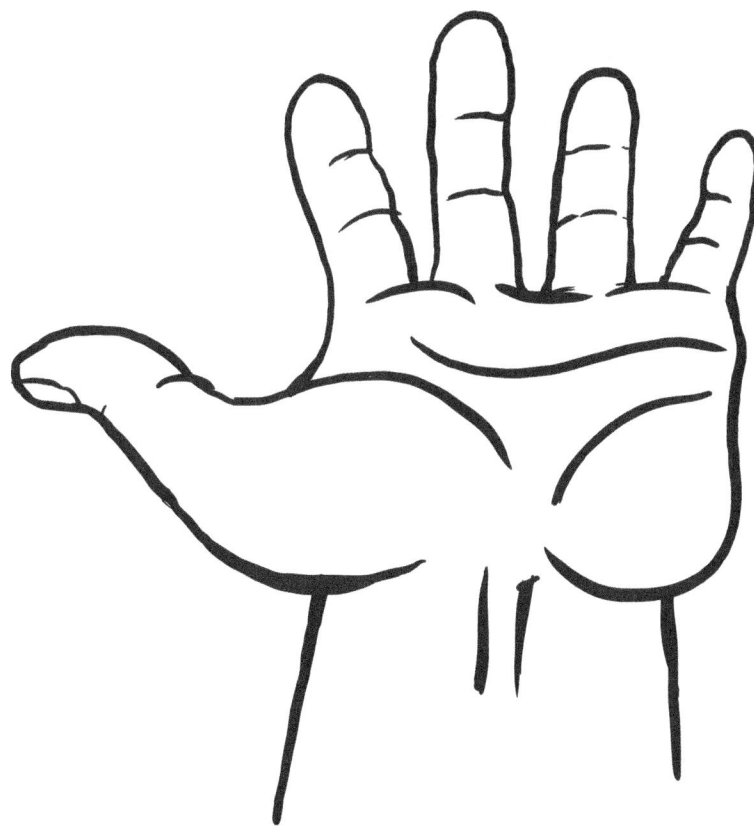

Figure 6.5 Maybe hand

Encouraging children to use the 'maybe hand' where appropriate establishes a positive kinaesthetic anchor – a mental link between the physical act and the good feelings that come from understanding a how-to mode of thinking that generates a number of ideas (none of which is necessarily correct), thus diminishing the fear of getting it wrong in some children's minds. You are also encouraging them to think in multiples, to have a number of ideas to reflect on further rather than settling on or grabbing at the first idea that comes to mind. This 'first-snatched-thought syndrome' is a lazy way of thinking and often shows up in children's writing as a chain of and-thens, a loosely linked sequence of the first ideas that came to mind. To be sure, the ideas might link logically to form a decent plot, but they are likely not the strongest ideas the child could have thought of if given a little more time to reflect.

Demonstrating the maybe hand also creates the opportunity to raise the matter of how likely the various explanations might be. In most people's worldview (we presume), it's more likely that the light is a firework than a dragon's fiery breath.

- Collect as many maybe-ideas as possible and ask the children to note them along a continuum, from highly unlikely (or impossible) to very likely. Discuss the reasons for sequencing them in this way.

During one workshop a child said, 'But if this was a scene from a Fantasy movie, then it's more likely that the light is a dragon's fiery breath, rather than a spaceship'. Here you can introduce or revisit the if-then pattern of thinking. If X is the case, then Y becomes possible and Z becomes much more likely because …

Sometimes a child says, 'Well I think that's an ugly cat', which may be something of a mental knee-jerk reflex rather than a considered view. Here you can credit the child with noticing the cat but point out that he also gave an opinion about it. By doing this you've separated out an observation from a value judgement/opinion.

And then you move on. Framing your response in this way achieves the following:

- You've allowed the child to have his opinion.
- You've offered sincere praise for his observation.
- You've not 'bought into' any agenda of confrontation he might have in mind if he said it just to try and annoy you.
- You've made the point (to the whole class) that there is a difference between an observation and an opinion.
- You've pointed out that opinions can vary.
- You've maintained your dignity and control over the flow of the lesson!

It's beneficial to cultivate this separating-out as a habit of thought since when observations and unconsidered opinions remain glued together (so-called obserpinions), they can become generalised and build up a strong emotional charge. For example, during a bus journey we recently overheard someone say that he 'hated the Welsh' because a crowd of Welsh football fans had laughed and cheered when their team scored a goal against their English opponents. It was troubling that the person in question used such an extreme term as 'hate' but also that he said it with real anger.

A way of preventing the build-up of such generalisations, or of teasing them apart if they are already established, is to ask some detailed questions, often using the what-if pattern of thinking:

- What if a person had been born in Wales but moved to England when he was a baby. Would you hate him as much as someone who is Welsh born and bred and still lives there?
- What if someone who has lived in Wales was a staunch England supporter? How would you react then?
- What if half the players on the England side had been bought by the Welsh manager and vice versa; how would you feel then about each team?
- What if a person was born at home in a house that straddled the Welsh-English border? Would you hate that person half as much as you hate someone who was born entirely in Wales?
- What if you discovered that an acquaintance of yours, born and raised in England, had suddenly become interested in football and supported the Welsh national team? Would your feelings towards him or her change? Why?

It goes without saying that we didn't challenge our Welsh-hating fellow passenger – partly because some people can feel threatened or foolish when their prejudices are challenged in this way and may react angrily. And indeed if the 'ugly cat' comes up as you explore the picture, you can make the point about obserpinions without requiring the children to reveal or defend any of their own.

CHAPTER

Questioning with confidence

Show the children the picture in Figure 7.1 and ask them to come up with as many questions as they can within two minutes. The aim is to encourage questioning as a habit, as an intelligent expression of curiosity rather than an expression of ignorance.

Follow up by inviting the children to ask as many questions as possible within a time limit about some ordinary object such as a pencil. Take the activity further

Figure 7.1 Heavy seas

by doing a question analysis to look at different kinds of questions. Categories of questions might include the following:

- open or closed
- questions that can be easily answered
- questions that are more difficult to answer
- questions that have answers but ones which can't be known
- questions that have no answers

Children might want to add categories of their own: scientific questions, funny questions, really interesting questions, etc.

Take the activity further by revisiting the 'big open question words' of where, when, what, how, who and why. Pick one of these and instruct children to ask only questions beginning with the chosen question-word.

Tip: Use an anchor (see page 114), such as a large question mark during these activities, to signal to the children that it's fine for them 'not to know' and that you approve of them asking questions. Be sure to use the anchor again during science lessons, when you study a story or poem, etc.

As the French philosopher Voltaire said (paraphrasing), judge people by the questions they ask rather than the answers they give.

CHAPTER

Collecting motifs

A motif is a constituent feature of a picture, text, etc., that helps to define the mood or genre of the whole piece. A motif can be a person, object, setting, section of dialogue or sequence of events. Helping children to notice motifs has the following benefits:

- The activity helps to focus the attention, develops observational skills and invites children to describe what they've noticed.
- Increasingly, children are challenged to explain how or why the motif they've noticed contributes to the mood or tone of the picture or helps to define the genre.
- The activity serves as a precursor to talking about motifs as part of an analysis of images, text, film and other media.
- Collecting motifs also helps to reinforce the 'show don't tell' principle important in narrative (page 81). Asking children to notice what 'clues' contribute to the mood of an image allows them to put the same kinds of details into their own work when they want to create a similar mood.

So using our 'cat on the corner' picture again, motifs would include the following:

- a lonely street
- darkness and gloom, shadows
- a cloudy sky
- a frightened or angry cat
- recent rain
- bare trees, an autumn look
- a few leaves blown by the wind
- a mysterious light in the sky

Once children have noticed these and made them explicit, complete the following:

- Ask how they contribute to the mood of the picture. How would children describe the mood? (There can be various answers to this: gloomy, spooky, scary, lonely, etc.) Children can use a thesaurus to help them here. If they do, ask them to think about subtle differences in the meanings of the terms they find. How is 'spooky' different from 'scary' for example?
- Extend the activity by combining it with the 'beyond the frame' exercise on page 70. Having noticed some motifs and described the mood or tone of the picture, what other *imagined* details would reinforce the atmosphere – a shadowy figure standing under a streetlamp, the clatter of a tin can in a nearby alley, a sudden rain shower blowing down the street, etc.
- You can revisit the activity after children have tried the multisensory-thinking exercises that follow. Adding colours, sounds, textures and feelings to the list highlights the mood of the picture even further.
- One class created a wall display of motifs. This took the form of clip art images, pictures cut from comics or drawn by the children, keywords and phrases. It was very colourful and provided an at-a-glance reference when the children were writing.

Figure 8.1 Space romance

Collecting motifs

Figure 8.2 Knocking on the door

Figure 8.3 Hut on the cliff

- Show some written motifs (such as those in the previous list describing the cat on the corner) to a group that hasn't seen the picture from which they were prompted. What scenes do the children imagine?
- Play extracts of instrumental music. These might complement pictures you show the class, but in any case they can serve as the basis for talking about mood and atmosphere. Extend the activity by looking at video clips that combine pictures and sounds to create mood.
- Use motifs to suggest a title or theme for a picture and use that as the theme in a subsequent story. So the title/theme 'cat on the corner' or 'lost', etc., can form the basis of a story that need have nothing to do with the image that inspired it.

What motifs can the children spot in Figures 8.1–8.3?

We hope to have demonstrated by now that using a simple picture allows you to introduce and practise a range of thinking skills with the children. From there you can move into other ways of using the imagination.

CHAPTER

Colour combinations

- Say to the class, 'Pretend this picture is in colour. Turn up the colours in your mind and when you've seen at least one colour, you can tell me what you've noticed'.

Again, be aware of how you've framed the task.

Figure 9.1 Cat on the corner 2

- The 'turning up' metaphor implies control.
- 'When' is a presupposition of success – you're sure the children will do it.
- 'Can' suggests capability and choice.

A number of children will respond immediately to this, demonstrating their ability to think visually. We receive impressions of the world through all of our senses, though over time some people tend to become more visually oriented thinkers: using that sensory mode over others becomes a habit. (You may notice that others in the class look a little confused or seem to be struggling to carry out the task. We'll deal with them later.)

Begin to collect colours from those volunteering their thoughts. Look out for the following:

- Would-be thinking (conditional thinking). Some children are tentative about what's on their minds. 'Well, lots of the leaves would be brown at this time of year'. Here the child is perhaps 'hedging her bets' by inferring the colour brown because of clues in the picture rather than having a direct mental experience of brown. Respond by saying, 'Throw away the would-be. *See* the colour of the leaves in your imagination and when you have, let me know'.

Framing it in this way uses 'when' as a presupposition of success. Consciously the child might not have realised this but subconsciously is likely to have registered your high expectations of her completing the task. Now the child might say, 'Yes, the leaves are brown'. Check that visual thinking is going on – 'Look again. Imagine that the leaves are not all the same colour. Notice this and tell me about it'. Many people, when asked to look inward in this way, will shift their eyes away from you. This is a further indication that the child is not just thinking 'intellectually'. (If the child finds it hard to visualise colours and is just trying to join in, don't push the issue; her visualisation skills will improve with practice.)

Incidentally, 'could be', 'might be', 'maybe', 'perhaps' in this context are all versions of tentative would-be thinking, often reflecting a lack of confidence or anxiety about being wrong. The maybe thinking we looked at on page 16 on the other hand (pun intended) develops confidence and creativity.

- Highlight the language. Commenting on the words children use when sharing their impressions heightens their awareness of and sensitivity to the language. It's another way of developing metacognition: when children reflect on a mental impression linked to the words they've used to express it, they deepen their understanding of the fact that changing the language refines or alters the imagery, and vice versa. Collecting ideas from a number of children reinforces the point that there's no single right answer and indeed that the notion of 'right answers' in this context is of limited value. However, if a child comes up with an unusual response, 'my leaves are rainbow coloured' for instance, point out that if she chooses to use that idea in a story or poem for example, then the leaves would be multicoloured for at least one good reason within the context of the writing. Also see the 'purple cat' anecdote on page 32.

CHAPTER

Subtle distinctions

Exploring the cat on the corner picture again, children often respond by saying, 'Well I see the leaves as reddish-yellowish'.

You can now feed back what the child has done, lacing your response with some sincere praise – 'Well done; you're not a lazy thinker. Instead of giving me just one colour word, you've joined two together. This gives my imagination more to work on. And you've altered the endings: you said red-ish and yellow-ish. So what do you think the difference is between a leaf that's reddish and one that's red?'

A number of children are likely to want to respond. A common distinction is that red is a 'solid' colour while reddish is a 'mixture' or 'blending' of shades. The children are now mentally paying attention to more subtle features of the leaf's colour while realising that this can be expressed in a number of ways.

Some children offer more detailed descriptions of the leaf once this step has been taken – 'I see my leaf with patches that are still green, but some are yellow shading into red, with a brown edge'. A positive reply to a description of such quality is to say, 'You know, if you wrote that in a story for me, I'd give you a big tick in the margin'. Or whatever your reward system might be. Of course, it's now possible that a number of children will want to earn their big tick by describing a leaf in that way or similar ways in their work!

Most children by now realise that you are sincerely interested in what they think and that what they think isn't 'wrong' but 'individual', one among a number of possibilities. So common replies can be as follows:

- I see a red leaf with yellow around the edges. (You can say, 'I like the detail of that idea'.)
- My leaf is red with browny-yellowy spots. (You can say, 'Oh, you've done the same thing but put an "ee" sound on the colour words instead of an "ish" sound. I like that too'.)
- In my mind, there are lots of leaves all blowing about in the wind so that lots of colours are flickering in front of my eyes. (You can say, 'Look what you did!

You've made me imagine movement; you've used a plural – colours – so that my imagination has to make lots of leaves. And I like that word you chose, "flickering", which is a really strong verb. So well done'.)

Responses like these mean that as well as valuing the children's thinking generally, you're feeding back to the whole class little 'linguistic tricks' for getting their imaginations working and for including subsequently in their writing. Make these learning points explicit:

- Simple details are effective.
- There's usually more than one way of creating an effect (ee as well as ish).
- Multisensory thinking (here, colour and movement) enriches what we can imagine.
- Plurals also prompt the imagination to do more work.
- (And more implicitly) The use of vagueness creates 'mental space' where the listener or reader can fill in the details.
- Choice of words is preferable to grabbing at the first thought that comes to mind.
- Giving clear concrete examples of more abstract concepts ('flicker' is a strong verb).

These linguistic techniques are also often criteria of quality in the use of language, supporting a larger principle than the plain, simple, clear expression of ideas that causes the listeners' or readers' imagination to do plenty of work is a measure of effective writing.

As children share their impressions, you can, of course, use the ideas to extend their understanding further. So, for instance, consider the following:

- Combining colour words. What other colour combinations can you use to describe the leaves? How many colour words can you string together before the impact is lost? (I can see a brownish-reddish-orangey-greeny-yellowish-terracotta-coloured leaf!) Point out that overuse of adjectives is to be avoided: it is an aspect of overwriting, which is a stylistic weakness.
- Exploring subtle differences. Is there a difference between a reddish-yellowish leaf and an orangey one? Is a pale yellow leaf the same as a light-yellow leaf?
- Testing understanding. If a child says, 'I can see a magenta leaf', ask him and the class if they can imagine that colour. Or ask for more detail about the colour. What does magenta actually mean? What things do you know that are usually coloured magenta? Can you see any examples of magenta in the classroom? A paint colour chart from a hardware store can be a useful resource here. Also point out that children should only use words they understand: a child may have heard the word magenta but have no idea what colour it represents.

There's also the opportunity here for children to research the etymology of some of the words they use. Magenta for example derives from the Italian city of the same name, where a battle was fought in 1859 shortly before the red dye was discovered (ref: *Oxford Dictionaries*).

- Challenging cliché. Sometimes a child will say that the sky is 'jet black'. In which case ask where the 'jet' comes from. Why do we say 'jet black'? And what about 'pitch black'? As well as creating an opportunity for research, it can challenge children to think beyond the obvious and come up with fresher descriptions. That said, encourage children to check any words they aren't sure about *after* they've completed a first draft: constant checking while writing interrupts the flow of ideas.
- Drawing out more detail. Encourage children to give you more information by asking 'what kind of?' as a response to what they say. So let's go back to the reddish-yellowish leaf; you can say, 'What kind of reddish-yellowish?' This prompts the child to revisit the imagined leaf and look for more to say:

Pupil: Well, a dry reddish-yellowish leaf.

You: What kind of dry?

P: Sort of, um, a bit crumbly.

Y: What kind of crumbly?

P: (rubbing the imaginary leaf between his fingers) Sort of flaky. It's coming to pieces, like in little papery bits...

Y: That's great. We have a reddish-yellowish leaf that's dry so that it crumbles into little papery bits. I really like the way you turned paper (noun) into papery (adjective).

On another occasion, a boy who rarely contributed offered the idea that he saw the sky as blue. Bearing in mind that the root of the word education means to 'draw out', the following conversation was of benefit to everyone:

Teacher: So what kind of blue do you imagine?

Pupil: Not dark but not too light. A kind of middle blue.

T: I don't think I've heard that before, 'middle blue'. What kind of middle blue?

P: Um . . . (looking around for an example, he then pointed to a countryside scene on a calendar pinned to the wall). That kind of blue.

T: Yes, but I want you to say it in words. People who read your work won't have that picture to look at. (The child went and looked more closely at the calendar.) 'What do you notice about it now?'

P: It's in the country. It's June. There's no clouds.

In the end, with only a little help, the child was able to say that the sky was a 'cloudless in-the-middle-of-nowhere June blue' and received a merit point for that startling description.

Another way of investigating colour is to explore the associations colours have, aspects of which involve the following:

- Cross-matching sensory impressions – synaesthesia – see page 62.
- Linking colours with moods and emotional states.
- Metaphorical thinking as we connect colours with signs and symbols.
- Discussing the importance of colour across different cultures.

We'll look at these in more detail later.

Incidentally, a number of the children will use hand movements as they describe the picture and its colours. You can point this out (although some children will become self-conscious about it) or, more elegantly, model the behaviour by using hand movements yourself as you describe details of the picture. So if you talk about crunching leaves you might be tempted to crumble some up in your hand. Or if you snap a branch you might find yourself doing this action as you describe it.

This is a rich area of exploration in the way we use our imaginations, and we'll look at the idea in more detail on page 41. Also, see the story of Billy and the apple on page 47.

- You can raise awareness of the link between physical movement and thinking by setting children the task of mentally and physically responding to a sequence of words and phrases you offer them: a firework exploding, trees swaying in the wind, a sheet of newspaper tumbling down the street, a gate creaking, a cat suddenly startled/frightened/angry.

Take it further by showing the children how to link their thinking with improvisation and other dramatic techniques. See Baldwin (2003).

Because the reddish-yellowish trick earned some praise, other children might now want to imitate. So you might get 'The sky is bluish-blackish' (sweeping a hand upward) or 'The pavement is greyish and whitish' (planing a hand across the horizontal). Accept several of these before moving on – because otherwise everyone might want to have a go! You can, of course, let them if time permits.

Sometimes a child might try to subvert the activity. One boy came up with, 'Well I can see a purple cat'. It's tempting simply to reject the idea, pointing out that cats are not purple. However, keeping the principle of utilisation in mind you can offer a more useful response – 'Well, your mind has given you that idea. But if you *choose* to use it in a story, then the cat would be purple for a good reason that would improve the story. So think about that and when you have a good, strong reason, let us know'.

Several things have been achieved here:

- You've saved the child some embarrassment by not rejecting his idea. He can now step away from the challenge without making a reply.

- You've reinforced the importance of thinking time. First-snatched-thought thinking is not a skill as such.
- You've communicated the message that we have control and choice when we write – i.e. we don't need to snatch at the first thought.
- You've highlighted the idea that things happen for reasons in a story, thereby touching on the notion of logical consistency in narrative.
- You've again used 'when' as a presupposition of success (page 27), motivating the child to reflect on his idea. You've also reinforced the notion that in the field of creative thinking it's fine to change your mind.

This last point is important since our expectations as teachers have a powerful influence on children's performance (see Rosenthal and Jacobson (2003)).

If you've previously touched on the idea of strength or likelihood of reasons (page 16), then now you can introduce a sliding scale of 1–6, where 1 indicates a reason that's not very likely or believable, while 6 means that the reason is robust and acceptable.

In the purple cat example, after about ten minutes the child put up his hand and told us that he knew why the cat was purple.

> Well the man who lives in the flat over there is a big Jimi Hendrix fan and he decided to paint his front room purple, to honour his hero. He went down to the shop and bought two big tins of purple paint. They were on offer. But coming home he slipped on some wet leaves and dropped one of the cans. That frightened the cat. Also, the lid popped open and splashed the cat with paint, and that's why the cat's purple.

Surely that's worth a big tick. Here the child created a believable narrative that linked several elements of the picture in a logical way and amused his classmates. What impressed us most though was that this 11-year-old knew about Jimi Hendrix!

With colours still in mind, but moving now towards sounds, children will often talk about the grey pavement or the brown bricks of the wall. Point out the pleasing nature of those words when saying them aloud. Older children will know about assonance and alliteration, to which we normally reply, 'Yes, we know what these patterns of sound are technically called but listen to how good they *sound* . . . Grey pavement. Brown bricks'.

This touches on the topic of euphony, the quality of words that are pleasing to the ear (see Bowkett (2017) for more discussion on this). Realising this, some children will now offer further and sometimes more elaborate examples: 'The wild wind whistles through the brown branches, while rainwater dribbles and streams down the wet walls'. You can credit these attempts of course while also reminding the children that allowing ideas to come to mind and trying to compose more finished sentences *at the same time* can be counter-productive.

Tip: Advise children that when they are editing and proofreading their work they should review it twice: once reading visually and once reading aloud. Not only will they spot more errors doing this, but they also become more experienced in recognising when sentences flow smoothly and when words clash clumsily.

CHAPTER

Sound work

At some point you can say to the class, 'You can still tell me about colours but also imagine the sounds coming out of the picture. Turn up the sounds, and when you've heard at least one you can tell us about it'. (Note that you can keep the picture exploration modular – notice and tell plus other kinds of thinking in one session, imagining colours in another, imagining sounds in a third, etc. The benefit of doing this is that the picture will become a positive visual anchor: each time you show it to the class you're building a link between the image and the pleasant experience of exploring it in these various ways.)

However, if you move straight into sound work and frame the task as we've suggested, notice how some children who have been eager to tell you about colours now fall silent. Their dominant sensory mode is likely to be visual. Other children who've told you about colours are still keen to tell you about sounds: it's useful to know that these pupils can do visual and auditory thinking with equal facility. Some of the children however now join in for the first time, indicating that their preference is to think in sounds. It may be that they gain a greater understanding when ideas and instructions are given to them orally rather than visually. Sometimes such children also talk to themselves as they try to work something out. This phenomenon has been called muttering the understanding or 'how do I know what I think until I hear what I say?'

So now you can explore sounds associated with the cat picture. Notice again how some children will use hand, arm and body movements as they articulate their thoughts. As children make their responses, challenge them further.

With regard to this and similar pictures, some children talk about the wind 'howling'. This is a cliché and most likely a first snatched thought – it's a common description and children will have picked it up without considering alternatives. Point out that we often describe wolves howling, so are there differences between the sound wolves make and the sound wind is making?

A child might of course say no, perhaps because he isn't listening carefully enough in his own imagination, or because he doesn't want to make the mental effort of exploring a distinction or because he sincerely thinks there is no difference. You can again use the principle of utilisation by opening up the task to the class or by offering an extension of the original task to the child in question: 'Imagine that the wind drops. It's not as strong or fierce now. How does that change the sound it makes?' This might produce some original thoughts such as; the wind is whimpering/the wind is crying.

- Explore subtle differences of sound. For instance, ask children to imagine water running along the gutter and going down the drain. What sounds do you hear?

Some will immediately reply 'drip drop'. This is perhaps another first snatched thought, an off-the-peg response. Challenge this by suggesting that now more water is running along the gutter and going down the drain. Or imagine that it's just started raining and the underground pipe that carries the water away is dry, so what sounds do you hear as the first water hits that dry surface?

Take it further:

Another technique you can offer the children, which incorporates several of the ideas we've looked at (and listened to), is to point out the relationship between sounds, letter patterns and tactile impressions. For example, consider the following:

- Pretend there are four puddles nearby. They all look the same. You've got four small stones in your hand and you drop one into each puddle. The first makes the sound *splish*, the second *splash*, the third *splosh*. What do you think is the difference between the puddles? What sound do you think a stone dropped in the fourth puddle would sound like? What if there was a fifth puddle that followed the sequence?

Have you noticed that the 'sp' sound is often used in words that talk about water? Let's make a list ... spit, spatter, spray, spurt, splat, splootch, spittle, spotting or spitting (with rain), etc. What kind of movement of the water is suggested by these words?

As children think about this, in their minds they will be linking the physical act of dropping the pebbles and the texture and hardness of the stones with the sounds they make when dropped into water. Reinforce this idea by telling children that there's a low wall up the road topped by metal railings. The children run by and drag a stick along the railings. What sound does that make? Then they run by again but this time with a metal rod. How is the sound different?

- And I've noticed that the hard 'c' and 'r' sound – cr – makes me want to clench my hand when I say crush, scrunch, crack, crumble, crackle, crinkle, etc.

The value of doing this is as follows:

- It rehearses words the children know and makes significant links between them.
- Gives children practice in multisensory thinking.
- Reinforces the ethos that playing with words is a learning experience.

Extend the activity by asking the children themselves to come up with other scenarios that encourage imagining sounds and linking them to physical movement.

- This is an ideal opportunity to introduce or revisit onomatopoeia. Some onomatopoeic words are likely to come along anyway and again prompt children to think further. If a child says the firework goes 'bang' (notice the hand movements), ask him to imagine someone lighting the fuse; what sound does that make (the click of a lighter, the rasp of a match on the sandpaper strip)? Then there's the sudden flare and acceleration as the rocket flies upwards. Or glowing orbs shooting out of a Roman candle – what sound do these make? Then after the explosion, there's the cascade of sparks. What do they sound like? And often, there are other sounds (like whistlings and screechings); ask the children to describe these to you.
- Sometimes children spontaneously make up new words to describe sounds. These may be combinations of known onomatopoeic words, but occasionally they are original. Ask the class what could be making these sounds (not necessarily connected to the picture); wizzooo, blap, donkk, thup, shuff-uffer, timble, zank, duh-luh-duh (our spell checker red-underlined every one of these!). Simple activities like this help to develop phonemic awareness (and in a fun way!).
- Using a variety of small objects, ask children to describe the sounds they produce. Drop a marble onto a plastic tabletop. Shake a metal cup with a coin in it and then add more coins. Draw your finger down a condensation-fogged window. Scrunch up a handful of 'packing peanuts' (polystyrene pieces). Tap different objects against the same surface. How do the sounds differ?
- Show the class short video clips without sound and ask the children to imagine and tell you about the sounds associated with them. A line of racing cars zooming by. A glass smashing. Empty tin cans bouncing down a flight of stone steps. A rocket launch. People diving into a swimming pool. Play the clips again with the volume up and ask the children how their ideas matched the actual sounds. What other sound words linked to the video have they now noticed?
- Link shapes and textures with sounds. Ask for examples of round sounds, spiky sounds, flat, heavy, light, sharp, smooth, rough prickly, wet, dry, cold, hot and pointy sounds. (Accept both conventional and made-up words.)
- Do a short 'sound meditation' with the class. Ask the children simply to sit quietly and notice sounds going on around them. Instruct the children not to make any sounds themselves. The act of sitting quietly just listening can itself have a deeply calming effect. Afterwards ask what sounds the children heard.

You can take this further by investing in a Tibetan singing bowl. These usually come with a striker: a short stick sometimes padded with leather at one end. Rubbing the striker around the rim of the bowl creates a beautiful ongoing tone. Or you can tap the bowl with the striker and ask the children to listen as the note fades, pinpointing the moment when it vanishes into silence. Again, this is a quick and easy way to help the children to settle and relax. Used repeatedly over time, the sight and sound of the bowl form a positive visual and auditory anchor (also see for example page 35).

- If possible, extend the sound work by going on 'sound safaris'. School trips are ideal for this. Spare five or ten minutes and ask the children to settle themselves, standing or sitting quietly as they listen to the variety of sounds going on around them.
- Focus attention on categorising sounds, building the children's ideas into association webs. What sounds are associated with metal, wood, glass, plastic, water, fire, stone?
- Look at comics and extracts from text-based stories and pick out sound references. Superhero comics in particular are full of great onomatopoeic words.
- Show children lists of sound-related words and ask them to give you examples of what might make them.
- Draw these activities together by exploring the submodalities (components) of sound: volume, pitch, duration, timbre or tone. You can return to the example picture for this, combining it with the 'stepping-in' technique described next.

For more ideas, see the worddreams.wordpress.com URL in 'References and Resources'.

As we've mentioned, these sound-related exercises of the imagination help to develop children's phonemic awareness and, importantly, through the medium of wordplay. This term suggests an ethos of exploration, experiment and enjoyment when working with language. Encouraging children to play with sounds raises their awareness of how sounds are combined to form words and gives insight into how the sounds of some words are related to their meanings. The 'fun factor' is important in developing children's confidence when working with and learning more about language. Also, perhaps implicitly, wordplay gives children a sense of ownership of words and language. Language belongs to us no less than it belongs to Shakespeare, even if perhaps we haven't mastered it to the same degree.

Note: For a more formal and rigorous explanation of how phonemes are related to reading development, see McGuinness (1998).

- Playing with sounds.

It's easy to set up little 'sound scenarios' and then ask the children what they hear. More auditorily adept thinkers will probably get spontaneous impressions immediately, while children who are not so used to thinking in that way will have to make more of an effort of the imagination to hear the sounds. So you can suggest things like the following:

A sports car races up the road. Then a motorbike goes by. What differences do you hear between the two engines?
Sudden strong gusts of wind rush through the trees.
Someone is walking towards you along the street. Notice the sound of their footsteps.
A small aeroplane flies low over the houses.
Some empty milk bottles fall over on a doorstep nearby.

Tip: Allow children to make up their own sound words for this activity if they want to and urge them not to worry about spellings at this stage if they write them down.

CHAPTER

Submodalities

The submodalities of a sensory mode are the aspects of the mode that make up the experience.

Visual:

Brightness – dim – bright
Size – large – small
Colour black and white – colour
Movement – fast – slow – still
Distance – near – far
Focus – clear – fuzzy
Location

Auditory:

Volume – loud – quiet
Tone – bass – treble
Pitch – high – low
Tempo – fast – slow
Distance – close – far
Rhythm
Location

Kinaesthetic:

Intensity – strong – weak
Area – large – small
Texture – rough – smooth
Duration – constant – intermittent
Temperature – hot – cold
Weight – heavy – light
Location

CHAPTER

Step in – the physical dimension

Once you've encouraged children to imagine colours and sounds, invite them now to step into the picture: 'Imagine you're going through a doorway. Step in and stand on that pavement so that you can notice all kinds of other things'.

'Notice' is a vague enough term to include tactile impressions, smells and tastes as well as further colours and sounds. Again, some children who have actively taken part up until now might have nothing further to say (yet), while others who may not have been very involved suddenly come up with a rich variety of details. Such children, whose tactile or kinaesthetic thinking is more highly developed, will often use big gestures and more overt body language as they tell you what they are thinking about. Their references will be predominantly physical: 'Well I stepped into the picture, and it's really cold (hugs herself). And the wind is strong (hand movements to indicate direction), and it's raining hard (jiggles fingers above head or mimes lashing rain hitting the face). And I stroked the cat (makes stroking movement), and it bit me (shows you which finger has been bitten)'.

It's not uncommon for children with 'tactile imaginations' to be quite fidgety in class, especially if they have been told to sit still, keep quiet and get on with their work (the classic three-part lesson plan!). The scope of this book doesn't allow for extensive discussion of the links between physical movement and learning, but key 'kinaesthetic learning' into your browser if you want to know more.

An important point to note is that while some children might have difficulty imagining textures and others sounds at the outset, by going through this sequence of activities with the whole class, every child is being given the opportunity and shown how to develop multisensory thinking. As the skill improves, benefits will come along in children's reading and writing. Predominantly visually oriented thinkers are more likely to load their creative writing with visual references, while there may be a lack of aural and tactile details. Thus, for a reader whose dominant mode is not visual, the work may seem 'thin', as though something is missing. However, as children gain the experience of using their imagination across different sensory modes, they will tend to put more multisensory references into their work (eventually beyond just prose fiction and poetry). Similarly, multisensory thinkers will enjoy a richer experience reading short stories and novels since they will have a greater awareness and appreciation of images, sounds and textures.

In the educational field known as accelerated learning, concepts and techniques touching on different sensory modes are collectively known as VAK – visual, auditory, kinaesthetic. Put 'VAK learning' into a search engine for heaps of information about this.

In the same way that you have focussed children's attention inwardly and explored more details of colour and sound, so you can now do this with textures, smells and tastes.

Invite all the children to reach out and touch something in the picture. Notice the ones who actually put out their hands to do this. Collect impressions and draw out further detail by trying the following techniques:

- Refine the impression. A pupil might say, 'I touched the moss between the stones in the wall and it was soft'. Reply, 'Well cotton wool and marshmallows are soft as well. What's the difference between the softness of the moss and the softness of cotton wool or a marshmallow?' You might now get 'damp softness', 'spongy softness', etc. One pupil said 'it's a green living softness' and got a big tick for that.
- Use the 'pretend-I-never' ploy. A child might say, 'I can smell the firework smoke in the air'. You reply, 'Pretend I've never smelt firework smoke. What words will you use to make me really *smell* that smoke now, in my nose?' You can open up the task to the whole class so that the burden (or rather joy) of thinking doesn't fall solely on the child who came up with the idea.
- Try the 'it reminds me of' ploy. This can involve association and simile. If you don't get a response using pretend-I-never, ask what the children are *reminded of* when they smell/imagine firework smoke. You'll probably get some obvious and conventional replies like Bonfire Night and New Year's Eve but also perhaps some fresh and startling ideas:

The smell of hot dead stars.
Fiery darkness and excitement.
It's like blue fog lying on my tongue.
Misty memories after the sparkles.
Echoes of yells and screams and laughter in my nostrils.
Sulphur smell, stinky and a kind of disappointment that the fireworks are over.
The cold, tingly, metally smell of that particular night.

Actually, what's important here is not whether the children come up with striking impressions, but that they are making the effort to go beyond an obvious or first-thought response: you are encouraging them to *reach* for words that they may never have combined before, trying to express something in a way that's new for them.

Incidentally, an image that strikes the listener's or reader's imagination and has an emotional impact is called a vivid particularity. These linger in the memory for a long time. As you read with the children, look out for startling images that evoke a strong sudden feeling. One of our favourites is found in H. G. Wells's classic *The Time Machine*. As the time traveller pushes the lever and begins to accelerate into the future, he notices that 'night followed day like the flapping of a black wing'. That still stirs the heart and the imagination with its promise of excitement, danger and the adventure of going where no one has gone before, boldly or otherwise.

Our experience has been that most children can remain engaged for a long time as you go through the picture exploration process. Even the fidgety (kinaesthetic) members of the class stay with you. One reason for this is that when we imagine carrying out some physical activity, the same areas of the brain are active as when we do it in the real world. At the level of neurons, the brain does not distinguish between fantasy and reality (that statement opens up a huge philosophical can of worms!). The phenomenon is well-known, to the extent that many athletes, as part of their training, visualise themselves again and again performing at their peak. As the brain responds, electrical impulses travel down through the body and trigger micro-movements in the muscle fibres. This is in effect a specialised application of how our thoughts, feelings and physiology are intimately connected. It's called training the neurology. For more on this, try the sportsandthemind.com website.

CHAPTER

What's the feeling?

Quite commonly, children (not just tactile thinkers) will offer an idea that is accompanied by a feeling. It's worth spending a little time on this, as it focusses children's attention on the way thoughts, emotions and physical sensations are connected, preparing the ground for the kind of emotional resourcefulness work we look at on page 161.

So using this picture, a child might say, 'I think these woods look spooky. Maybe they're haunted'.

Figure 14.1 The Lonely Forest

There are various things that you can do at this point.

You might say, 'What is it about the woods that makes you say that?' Or, 'Notice what's going on in your body to give you that spooky feeling'.

You can also use pictures like this to discuss atmosphere and mood. Insights can then be applied to the study of text. As a bridge to this, ask children to write a short descriptive piece about the woods, using what they've learned about multisensory thinking. They can prepare for this by simply noting impressions in a stream-of-consciousness way, allowing ideas to pop into mind without making any attempt to organise them or compose the piece of writing.

Other reasons why most children concentrate for long periods when using their imaginations to explore pictures are as follows:

- It doesn't feel like work.
- It's enjoyable and different.
- Children feel safe (i.e. not afraid they'll look foolish by giving a wrong answer).
- The activities are inclusive; everyone is invited to join in.
- The work is not comparative/competitive, unlike with much of the curriculum.
- Children feel a sense of ownership as they contribute their thoughts.
- The work invites active participation, not the passive receiving of facts.
- At this stage anyway, the work doesn't involve much writing (yet lots of thinking).
- Children are credited for performing at their current level of ability – differentiation by outcome.

CHAPTER

Two anecdotes

Here are a couple of stories that help to illustrate the points listed earlier.

The boy who thought of the purple cat (page 32) is Tyler. His teacher told us that he was a 'disaffected learner' who rarely got involved in classroom activities if he didn't have to. She was surprised and pleased that he did some thinking in response to our query of why the cat was purple. Following his reply, Tyler became more interested in the picture exploration but was still fidgeting, so we gave him an individual task to carry out:

> Tyler, we're sending you on a mission. If you choose to accept it, climb over the wall, jump down the other side and cross the garden to the tree that's growing close to the house, but watch out for the guard dogs prowling around. Scramble up the tree until you come to the stout branch that almost reaches the open first-floor window. Crawl along the branch carefully because it can only just take your weight. Get into the house and search for the secret plans that are hidden there somewhere. Beware of the guards on patrol. Return with the plans and two other interesting items. You can take any equipment you like. When you get back, tell us about your adventure.

At this, Tyler became still and quiet, with a look of concentration on his face. We didn't want to keep the rest of the class waiting, so we moved on with the workshop. Five minutes later Tyler became animated again, so we paused while he told us in detail about the dangers he'd faced carrying out his mission, how he'd dodged machine gun fire, a number of evil black-clad ninjas, stun grenades and other horrors. He could even describe the interior of the house and the rooms he'd searched before finding the safe containing the plans. The merit point his teacher gave him was well deserved.

The value of this task is as follows:

- It gives practice at internalising the attention and noticing the flow of one's thoughts (metacognition).
- It develops the concentration span in such a state (the state of 'relaxed alertness' characterised by alpha rhythms in the brain).
- It gives the child access to material that he can then report back, thus contributing usefully to the lesson.
- It shows him a technique for stilling the body that could act as a precursor to guided visualisations and guided meditation.

Billy's teacher described him as a 'reluctant writer' and told us not to expect much work from him. The focus of the workshop was descriptive writing, and the task we chose was to have the children describe an apple. Billy folded his arms and stared hard at his table, as though he was sulking. We decided not to press the matter because being forced to write is not the way to cultivate an interest in, let alone a love of, writing.

Glancing at him a couple of minutes later, we realised that Billy actually wasn't sulking; he was staring intently at something on the table – except there wasn't anything on the table. Moments later, he reached out and picked up the invisible object, turned it this way and that, sniffed it, polished it on his shirt, bit into it, wiped the juice off his chin, put the apple down and then started to write.

Usually, Billy's written work was cursory, but now he produced a paragraph that vividly described the size, shape, colour, texture, smell and taste of the apple. When we asked him how he managed to write such a mouth-watering description he said, 'Well when you write all of you has to do it', echoing the maxim that 'your imagination goes right through you' – mind, body and emotions all working together.

CHAPTER

Just enough

A vital aspect of writing is making decisions. This happens continually on a thought-by-thought, word-by-word and sentence-by-sentence level. One area of decision making in writing is choosing how much to put in and what to leave out. Writers have different working methods to tackle this. Some authors 'write it all out', putting in every detail they can think of and then discarding much of it during the second drafting (Steve's friend and mentor, the late Douglas Hill, called this 'hacking out the dead wood'). Some writers make copious notes beforehand and select as they go along. Some writers have developed the knack of writing sparely, relying on their readers' imagination to fill in details through shared experience. No method is inherently better than another; it's just what any writer feels is effective; the what-works-for-me principle.

You may well find that some children overwrite, putting in so much detail that the pace of the narrative slows and tension and drama are lost. This is sometimes the result of confusing quality with quantity. Others in the class (because they don't enjoy writing or for some other reason) write as little as they can. A useful rule of thumb is to put in just enough such that a reader can picture a character or scene clearly but can move through the story at a satisfying pace.

- Association web.

Take a phrase such as 'a fairground'. Put this in the middle of a large blank sheet and ask children to write around it things they associate with such a place. Remind them to use all of their senses to capture as much detail as possible (see the image on page 121).

Now ask the children to decide which details they would use in a short but vivid description of a fairground. They don't have to give reasons for their decisions, but you can credit them if they do.

- Descriptions on a postcard.

Give each child a standard blank postcard (A6 size, 148 × 105 mm or 5.8 × 4.1 inches) or sheet of paper about the same size. The task is to write a brief but vivid description of a fairground that ideally fits on one side of the card, though you can allow the writing to spill over onto the other side. Children don't need to use all of the details they selected from the association web.

Follow up by asking the class for more generalised phrases that can be used subsequently: a motorway service area, a Christmas market, a Halloween party, etc.

- Going beyond the limit (see also 'Beyond the Frame' on page 70).

There's a limited amount of visible detail in the following image (Figure 16.1), 'exploring the crypt'.

Use it in conjunction with the following:

1. Write the first sentence that comes to mind to describe the scene.
2. Now jot down what sounds, smells and textures the characters might experience.
3. What details that you can't see might be picked out by the torch beam?
4. Decide how the characters could be feeling (each character might have different emotions). Make a few notes about how someone could experience that

Figure 16.1 Exploring the crypt

emotion physically. So if a character feels nervous, maybe their hand will be trembling, the voice might sound shaky, they might move forward slowly and cautiously, etc.
5. Now either edit your first postcard piece or write another and more detailed description of the scene on a postcard, using the notes you've made.

CHAPTER

Sensory treasures

Most if not all of us have a favourite colour, object, smell, taste, etc. Give each child a scrap of paper and ask them to write down one of their favourite things, which might appeal just to one sense or to more. As a class activity, choose five or six examples each time you run the session. Read out the children's examples, leaving 15 or 20 seconds between each. You might want this to be purely a visualisation activity' or would prefer children to note their impressions.

Tip: To begin with, instruct children to concentrate as far as possible only on the object of that particular visualisation, ignoring associations and memories, and dampening the tendency to let the mind wander. Occasionally though, ask children to notice associated thoughts.

Note that as with all other visualisations, if any unpleasant thoughts or feelings arise, allow the child to open her eyes and find a distraction like reading a book or carrying out some other task.

Take it further:

The previous activity relies largely on assumed knowledge and shared experiences. If one of the examples was the smell of freshly brewed coffee, we'd assume that all of the children had smelt that at some time. Encourage children to speak out if this is not the case for any of the examples. (You might consider allowing children who haven't smelt fresh coffee, for example, to enjoy that experience some time.)

For those who have had the experience say, 'Pretend I have never smelt fresh coffee. What words would you use to give me an idea of that aroma?' Children will now be actively 'reaching' for vocabulary to express their impressions. This is not an easy task: using the sensory cross-matching technique (page 65) might help some children along.

In his book *The News: A User's Manual*, Alain De Botton recounts how the artist John Constable, between 1821 and 1822, would spend several hours each day carefully studying the ever-shifting colours, shapes and moods of the sky in order to create his beautiful watercolour, crayon and oil studies of skyscapes. Constable called this practice 'skying'. While we're not suggesting that many children would want to take things that far, as their ability to notice and concentrate develops they may well enjoy and find benefit from going outside simply to notice the skyline of the town against a backdrop of cloud, the movement of leaves in a gentle wind or the way clumps of flowers unfold from buds to full blooms from one day to the next (Ref: De Botton (2014), P211).

CHAPTER

Spelling strategies

Greater awareness of different sensory modes of thinking, coupled with the ability to concentrate inwardly while manipulating thoughts, opens up the possibility for children to try out different spelling strategies (and strategies for learning in other subject areas – see the reference that follows).

To illustrate this we'll mention Emily, a Year 5 pupil who was enthusiastic while we were asking the class to notice details in the sample picture but who seemed to struggle when we wanted the class to imagine colours. However, when we suggested that the children 'turn up the sounds in the picture' Emily immediately became animated and her hand shot up in the air as she now wanted to contribute.

'Oh, I can hear the cat meowing!' This was a kind of 'eureka moment' (see page 10), when an impression comes spontaneously to mind. Such sudden insights are invariably enjoyable: as we like to tell children, it *feels good* to have an idea.

We decided to focus on Emily for a while longer and said, 'That's great. Do something for me now please. Make the cat meow again and tell me, is it a long sound or a short sound?' Hands moving apart and then coming together served as a visual analogue to this mental task.

'It's a long sound', Emily said at once, her hands moving apart as she mirrored the gesture.

'Well done. Make the cat meow again. Is it a high sound or a low sound?' The voice going higher and lower as this was said, accompanied by a hand moving up then down.

'It's a high sound'.

'That's excellent. Now do this – listen to the very end of the next meow and tell me what you hear'.

Emily listened and a moment later said, 'The meow gets quieter and then stops'.

Such spontaneity is also a strong indication that, in Emily's case, she really is hearing the sounds in her imagination and not just naming them as an intellectual exercise. Another indicator is that children will sometimes look away from you as they see colours, hear sounds, etc. – their awareness is swinging inward so that you – an inhabitant of the outside world – cease to be the focus of their attention momentarily.

It was clear that Emily was highly adept at auditory thinking. She had mimicked our vocal tones so that as our voices went higher hers did the same a second later. Also she had the ability to listen to small and subtle details of sound in her imagination. The final question about the cat's meow confirmed this since she wasn't given an either-or, long-short/high-low option but was asked to notice whatever sound she heard.

Emily's ability is significant because it so happened she had a spelling problem. Her teacher had mentioned earlier that Emily was a very bright girl but that her spelling was 'holding her back'. Her particular behaviour was to transpose a couple of letters, usually in the middle of a word, as she tried to remember the spelling. 'Possibly she's dyslexic'[1], her teacher said, agreeing to work with us later so that we could find out a bit more.

Emily gave up her morning break so that we could work with her. We asked her to spell 'already', which had been on the previous week's spelling list. She wrote it from memory and it came out as 'alraedy'. We pointed out that the a and e were in the wrong positions and then said, 'Try this – pretend you've got a little toffee hammer in your hand. Tap those two letters and tell us when you know what sounds they make'. This was something she could do immediately. She pointed to the a and said *bing*, then at the e and said *plonk*. 'Bing-plonk'. She could easily remember the auditory structure for the error she'd made.

Then Emily wrote the word out again, and we made sure the letters were correctly sequenced. 'Tap with the toffee hammer so that so you know they're in the right place'. Emily said 'Plonk-bing', easily remembering the auditory structure for the correct positioning of the two letters that had caused the difficulty.

Note

1. Controversially but persuasively in her book *Why Children Can't Read – and What We Can Do about It*, Professor Diane McGuinness argues that dyslexia is a myth and that children's difficulties in reading, spelling, etc., are the result of 'teaching methods that are based on outdated and often harmful techniques' (from the cover blurb). Whether that raises a cheer or a growl of rage from you, we heartily recommend McGuinness's highly informative book.

CHAPTER

Break state

Immediately after Emily had used her toffee-hammer technique to fix the correct spelling of 'already' in her memory (see Section 18) we said, 'What's that outside?' and Emily looked through the window. This distraction technique is called a break state. For the past few moments Emily had been in an intense state of concentration learning a new strategy for remembering letter sequences. Once we'd taken her through the process, we broke that state of concentration. This acts as a mental full stop and says to the brain, 'That's all you need to learn now to be able to do it for yourself whenever you like'.

'It was a bird', Emily's teacher said. 'It's gone now'. Then we gave her a clean sheet of paper and asked her to write the word out again, 'Making sure you tap those letters you used to get wrong to be sure they're right'. Emily wrote out the word unhesitatingly and correctly.

Checking with her teacher some weeks later, we were told that Emily was still using the 'toffee hammer tap trick', as she called it (notice the lovely alliteration) to remember 'already' and was also using it to remember other words that she had struggled with previously.

It turned out that all of the children in that class had been taught the look-see-say-cover-write-check strategy for learning spellings. Apart from the 'say' bit, this is an entirely visual strategy but one that in Emily's case wasn't working very well. But by identifying how she preferred using her imagination, with a little thought we were able to suggest a new strategy that worked more effectively for her.

The technique doesn't just apply to sounds. Children who clearly imagine colours should have no trouble mentally seeing a word whose spelling might have caused some problems. They might well report that the letters of the part they get wrong are blurry or pale. Suggest giving each troublesome letter a different bright colour. Get the child to tell you when he's done that and then do a break state. Ask him subsequently to visualise the word again with those bright colours and write it out – you can even suggest he use coloured pencils to mirror what he sees mentally.

DOI: 10.4324/9781003184003-19

A further benefit of this kind of activity is that it's versatile and playful. Listening closely to sounds, turning up colours and mentally exploring textures doesn't feel like work. And because the children you work with can already do the kinds of thinking you're asking them to engage with, their confidence is likely to be high and they'll be more motivated to have a go.

In his excellent book *Dynamic Learning*, Robert Dilts (Dilts and Epstein (1995)) asserts that children who don't spell well 'aren't bad spellers. They just haven't found the right strategies yet'. Dilts goes on to examine how the elegant use of the imagination can help children with language learning, reading, creative writing, maths and various memory techniques.

CHAPTER

Minimal writing and artful vagueness

We made the point earlier that one reason some children take to the picture exploration work is because (so far) it hasn't involved much writing, though it does encourage a lot of focussed thinking and talking. In that sense the process itself is the point and 'product' of the lesson, its learning outcome. Obviously though, writing can follow on from what the children have done up until now. Techniques for encouraging children who don't normally enjoy writing include the following:

- Artful vagueness. This is one example of the more general principle of flexibility within a structure, where children are given a definite task, a how-to way of going about it and a defined outcome but are allowed enough creative space to make choices of their own. Note that Tyler (page 46) was told that the secret plans were 'somewhere' in the house and that he was to bring them back plus two other 'interesting items'. These artfully vague instructions meant that Tyler could decide for himself what the items would be and where the plans were hidden. Being too prescriptive when giving children writing tasks can inhibit their creativity, partly because they're too busy trying to concentrate on and follow all the instructions. Too little guidance can leave them floundering as they struggle to generate and sequence their ideas: 'I want you to write a story for me now, but don't worry I'll help you by putting the title on the board' is a classic example.
- Minimal writing. This is where you deliberately limit the amount of writing the children are to do. Versions of this include the following:
- Minisagas. These are tiny stories that must be exactly 50 words long, not including a title, which can contain up to 15 words. A minisaga should be a story (not a description) featuring a beginning, a middle and an end. Being so strict about the word count gives children the experience of editing and making every word do useful work. You can help by suggesting a theme and even a plot. Advise them just to write the story first without trying to hit the 50-word target, though obviously keeping the word count as low as possible, and then to trim the work to try and achieve exactly 50 words.

Vary the task by showing children a picture of a target, such as you'd use in archery. Point out that 50 words mean a bullseye, but that more words mean hitting the target farther away from the centre. Alternatively, you can ask children to write a 'midisaga' (100 words) or a 'maxisaga' (200 words) or your own variations of this idea.

- Chain stories. Show the class the synopses of several short stories broken down into a sequence of events. Split the class into as many groups as there are stories. Ask each group to decide which child will write first, who will write second and so on. The children in each group can help one another as the story passes down the chain and each child does her or his share of the writing. If the other children in a group are not helping out they can be getting on with some other task such as the following:
- Comic pages. Scan a story, or part of a story, from a comic book and erase the dialogue. The children's task is to fill in the speech bubbles, thought bubbles and text boxes with what they think the characters and narrator are saying. An alternative is to keep the dialogue but blank out some of the panels. The children then have to describe what could be happening in the blank panels (Figure 20.1).

In this example, Tanzie Tucker is helping her father Tony, a private detective, to work out who broke into a small service station and robbed the safe. Children can prepare for the task by

Making up names for the other characters.
Deciding what part those characters play in the story.
Imagining the pictures in colour and making notes.
Thinking about what earlier pages in the story would show.
Looking for clues to help decide who committed the crime.

- Also see writing on a postcard, page 49.
- Blackout poetry. Rather than throw battered old storybooks away, take out the pages and give each child or group a few to work with. Ask the children to scan-read the pages first and look for an anchor word – a word that suggests a topic and focus for the poem. Then read the pages in their entirety and lightly circle or underline any words associated with the anchor word. Avoid circling more than three words in a row. Now list the chosen words on a separate piece of paper, keeping them in the same order as they appear on the page of the story. Return to the page and erase the circles or underlining of any words you will not be using. Complete the blackout poem by scribbling out all but the chosen words. A picture can be drawn to accompany the poem. Look online to see some examples.

Figure 20.1 Deleted dialogue

Copyright material from Steve Bowkett and Tony Hitchman (2022), *Visualising Literacy and How to Teach It*, Routledge

Minimal writing and artful vagueness

If you key 'images of blackout poems' into a search engine you'll find plenty of examples to show the children before they begin. As you'll see, blackout poems can be very brief and are usually free verse, without rhyme, metre or verse pattern. And for any purists who think the blackout technique doesn't produce 'real' poems, we'll mention that the word derives from the Greek *poiein* 'create', something the children are self-evidently doing.

- Micropoems. A micropoem is just a few lines long with a syllabic pattern that you or the children can choose: 1 – 2 – 3 syllables, 2 – 3 – 4, etc. Having done some picture exploration work means that there is plenty of choice of topic. Such a poem can attempt to convey a sense of the whole picture or might focus on some small detail.

The best way to approach a micropoem once the topic or focus has been decided is to write it out first in 'normal' sentences, keeping them as brief as possible. Each line can be a separate statement (this works best), or words can flow from one line to the next, though the temptation here is just to write a sentence broken up into three lines, which diminishes the poetic quality of the piece. Cut out any words that do relatively little work – 'packing' words such as the, a, an – then tweak and polish until you are satisfied that the poem says what you intend it to say within the specified format.

So using our cat picture as an example, here's a pupil's first attempt at a 2 – 3 – 4 syllable poem:

The gate bolt
is rattling
like it's restless.

Trimmed down:

Gate bolt
rattling,
restless.

Tweaked and polished:

Gate bolt
so restless –
Rattling wind.

One strength of this finished poem is its musicality; the repetition of l and t sounds emphases the onomatopoeic/metallic quality of 'rattling', while the repetition of 'in' echoes the sound of the wind. The use of the em-dash marks a change of thought, a kind of shifting of attention away from the bolt itself to the larger phenomenon of the wind. The writer was also given credit for visualising the bolt, which is not visible in the picture.

Here are a few more examples from Year 6 children:

Frightened cat.
Sky explodes
this windy night.

Cat,
darkness,
stormy night.

Spongy damp moss
Smells of green autumn –
Life thrives between dead stones.

CHAPTER

Cross-matching senses

By and large we have kept the senses separate during the picture exploration work. However, there is a mental phenomenon called synaesthesia in which one sense is perceived through or expressed as another. (The word itself comes from the Greek meaning 'with' or a 'coming together of' sensations.) What we might call 'strong synaesthesia' is a neurological condition where the stimulation of one sense triggers reactions in another. A person with this ability might experience sounds as colours, or where ordered sequences such as numbers or the months of the year are perceived as having their own personalities (perhaps we've all experienced miserable Monday, but this kind of extreme personification-synaesthesia is rarer).

As a literary device synaesthesia is the technique writers use to present characters, places, objects or ideas such that they appeal to more than one sense. Consider this list of words: austere/backbone/big/crisp/earthy/firm/flabby/green/high notes/grip/lean/sharp/silky/soft/steely/undertones. We usually associate 'austere' with a certain manner or attitude, while 'high notes', 'sharp' and 'undertones' are linked with sound. However, all of these words are terms used by wine tasters to describe the smell and taste of wine.

This kind of synaesthesia is metaphorical and happens, you might say, intellectually. It is a common feature of everyday language. Thus we associate sound with colour when we talk about 'muted tones' or 'loud colours'; a 'frozen silence' links a physical sensation with sound (or lack of); 'bitter cold' cross-matches a taste with a tactile experience.

Introducing the idea to your class gives children another way of using their imaginations.

- Present the class with a sequence of sounds, one at a time. Ask the children to imagine that each sound tells us something about a person's character. What do we learn about that person each time a chosen sound is heard?

- Take it further. Play some instrumental music and say to the children, 'Pretend this music is describing a person. What does he or she look like, and what emotions is that person experiencing?'
- Gather up objects and materials with different textures. Invite the children to touch them. 'Imagine these textures are emotions. Which emotion goes with which texture?'

The cultural critic John Ruskin coined the term 'pathetic fallacy'. This is the attribution of human traits or emotions to objects and nature. So we can talk about a raging storm, the merciless desert sun, a gloomy day, bitter cold and so on.

Show the children the following lists of emotions and features of the landscape (Figure 21.1), ask them to cross-match to create further examples of pathetic fallacy. Where necessary asking for the reasoning behind the idea.

Emotions	Landscape Features
Affection	Beach
Anger	Cliffs
Anxiety	Clouds
Apathy	Crags
Boredom	Dunes
Concern	Earthquake
Courage	Flood
Curiosity	Forest
Delight	Glacier
Despair	Gorge
Disappointment	Heath
Dread	Hills
Enchantment	Island
Envy	Lake
Fear	Lightning
Fury	Marsh
Guilt	Moon
Happiness	Moorland
Horror	Mountains
Joy	Ocean
Loneliness	River
Love	Rock
Peacefulness	Stars
Rage	Storm
Sadness	Sun
Shock	Thunder
Sorrow	Valley
Terror	Volcano
Wonderment	Waterfall

Figure 21.1 Emotions and landscape features

Figure 21.2 Abstract shapes for character exploration

Take it further by imagining chosen emotions as a sound, a shape, a colour. What emotions might the following abstract shapes suggest (Figure 21.2)?

Incidentally, pathetic fallacy is a particular kind of personification, which is a broader term where human emotions are projected onto something non-human.

CHAPTER

Drawing out meaning

The term 'synaesthesia' can be used more generally to mean the ability we have to combine sensory impressions in the imagination or to express a sensory impression by borrowing language usually associated with other sensory modes.

As an example, a few years ago we did the jump-into-the-picture activity with a class and Sarah put her hand up at once. 'Oh, I can smell the fireworks!' she said, with that note of excitement that marks both a eureka moment and childlike enthusiasm, both of which are precious.

'Say more about that'.

But then Sarah frowned and started to struggle. 'Well, it's a kind of, um – a sort of a – of I don't know. It's quite a nice smell'. Because she couldn't find suitable words at that moment she fell back on a vague and clichéd response, essentially giving up on the task. One reason was that she had been struggling to find only 'smell words' to describe smell, but that's not really necessary.

'Imagine you can reach out and touch the smell[1]. When you can feel the smell, tell me what it's like'.

At this, Sarah's hand reached out as she concentrated on what was happening in her mind. 'It's soft and fluffy, like cotton wool', she said.

'Now imagine you could hear the firework smell. What does the smell sound like?'
'Like, kind of quiet and humming. . .'
'And give the smell a colour right now. What colour is that smell?'
'It's light purple', Sarah said at once.
'So tell us more about the smell of the fireworks. . .'
'It's a soft, fluffy, quiet, humming light purple smell'.

Not only was Sarah pleased with the fact that she'd 'done it', but she was delighted with the merit point her teacher awarded her for such a rich and original description of the smell of fireworks. Notice also how quickly Sarah responded: the mind works fast, especially when we allow spontaneous subconscious impressions to pop into the conscious mind rather than trying to carry out the task using only conscious effort.

This technique doesn't require you to teach children new words (although you can of course) but rather shows them how to use the vocabulary they already possess in a new way. And it's not about simply suggesting that a child can use touch words or sound words to describe smell; rather, give the child the experience of reaching out to touch, listening with the mind's ear and so on.

For more on synaesthesia, go to the https://faculty.washington.edu/chudler/syne.html website; for examples in literature, try literarydevices.net.

Note

1. Sometimes a child will tell you they can't do this. Rather than ask them to 'try', which suggests conscious effort and possible failure say, 'Well just pretend you can and tell me when you've done it'. That usually works fine. 'Just pretend' makes it safe because it's not real (though neurons don't know that) while 'when' is our old friend, a presupposition of success.

CHAPTER

Point of view

Once children have tried the 'stepping-in' technique as described on page 41, you can take the activity further in these ways:

- 'When I tell you, use your imaginations to step into the picture again, but this time I want you to pretend that you are a very frail and elderly person. As you stand on that street, what thoughts and feelings are you experiencing?'

Your instruction will prompt a memory search where children piece together bits of information associated with the notion of being elderly. Once they've had some thinking time, get them to step in and then after a minute or so ask for their impressions. Suggest to the class, or have the children suggest, different types of people for further stepping-in sessions. By encouraging them to see the world from another's point of view, you are developing empathy: the ability to experience vicariously what someone else might be thinking and feeling. The word comes from the Greek em- 'in' and pathos 'feeling'. Running the activity a number of times also develops the children's ability to 'get inside' the characters they feature in their stories. It also allows them to respond more sensitively and/or insightfully whenever you ask, 'How would *you* feel in that person's shoes?'

- Character creation. As well as jumping into a picture, get the children to 'jump into a person'. This might be an image of a character, or you can say, 'When you go into the picture today pretend to be (for example) an older person living alone. What thoughts and feelings do you have as you stand there on the pavement?'

This technique shows children a way of imaginatively engaging with a character in a more powerful way than asking them to 'think about the characters in your story'. 'Jumping in' works especially well if you have previously done the multi-sensory work described earlier. What does the character's voice sound like? Go into submodalities to draw out more detail (page 40). What does the person smell like – is she wearing perfume, or is he wearing body spray? What about the smell of soap or shampoo? (Also look at the notes on synaesthesia on page 65). What do this person's clothes feel like? What's their body posture as they stand there? What are their values, beliefs and opinions? (One way of approaching this last question is to ask the children to use abstract shapes or symbols to represent values and beliefs.)

As you'll see, this activity creates a bridge into role-play and improvisation work. Groups of children can jump into different characters and strike up off-the-cuff conversations. Also in-role, ask them to describe what their house or flat looks like, to describe their best friend, what they like to watch on TV, etc. (see Baldwin and Fleming (2003)).

Repeated jumping in to assume the mantle of different characters is a creative act because it encourages multiple perspectives. An older person living alone will have different thoughts and feelings as they stand on the street corner than those of a burglar on the lookout for an open window or a politician out canvassing for votes. The game gives children the experience of appreciating the world from somebody else's viewpoint.

- You don't need to do the stepping-in for this next activity, though by doing so the children might generate more ideas than they would otherwise. Pick a profession and ask what questions that person might ask if she were standing on that street. What questions might a historian ask? Or someone working in animal welfare? Or an estate agent? Invite children to come up with further professions.
- Still using the cat-on-the-corner image, choose a fictional genre and say to the class, 'When you step into the picture this time, pretend you're in a science fiction story (for example). What do you notice? What's going on?'

You have now created a mental 'filter' through which children will experience the picture based on their current understanding of the motifs (constituent features) and conventions (how they are normally used) of the genre. The light in the sky is now more likely to be a spaceship or perhaps a meteor plunging towards Earth. The cat could now have become an intelligent felinoid from the future who aims to reset time to ensure the survival of its species.

The technique can be used for various genres, though it helps if you have studied them previously with the class. A variation of the activity using this picture is to combine it with a topic: late Victorian England for example. When children step into the picture they will be reminded of some of the facts and ideas they learned about earlier.

- Be a character in a story you enjoy. Either step into the picture we've been studying – how would your character react to being there? – or imagine yourself as that character in the story he/she/it appears in. What comes to mind?

- Look at a page from a comic book. Now in your imagination, animate it – pretend it's live-action. You can experience it as though sitting in a cinema watching the movie or 'step in' and be part of what's happening.
- In the eclectic field of ideas and techniques known as neuro-linguistic programming, the use of perceptual positions or taking different viewpoints has various applications. Most usually, there are three positions: one's own, that of some other person and the 'objective observer' where you see, hear and feel yourself and others as though they were on a cinema screen.

The jumping-in activity where a child imagines he's an elderly person or a burglar, etc. (page 67), is a simpler version of the perceptual positions technique. In various situations to say to a child, 'How do you think (s)he feels about that?' is another. Using the technique most effectively requires a high level of self-awareness to utilize the first position, close and detailed observation of another person to appreciate the second position and a degree of sustained detachment to maintain the third.

The perceptual positions technique can help to overcome personal barriers and limits and to 'mirror' positive and successful patterns of behaviour that we notice in others. For more information on this, we recommend *Introducing Neuro-Linguistic Programming* (O'Connor and Seymour (1990)) by Joseph O'Connor and John Seymour and Michael Carroll's article at www.nlpacademy.co.uk/articles/view/using_perceptual_positions/.

CHAPTER

Picture masking

Choose a suitable picture and mask some of it from view. Ideally, the part of the picture that remains will feature clues as to what is no longer visible. Ask the class to look at the partial image carefully and then to suggest what might be found in the masked-off part. To do this they will need to speculate and infer. You can scaffold this activity by choosing pictures at the outset where it's relatively easy to infer what cannot be seen, working up towards more testing examples. Prompt ideas by encouraging children to ask open questions.

In our example (Figures 24.1–24.3), we reveal the full picture in stages. Take the activity further by going 'beyond the frame' or ask what might happen next.

Figure 24.1 What's going on here 1

Figure 24.2 What's going on here 2

Figure 24.3 What's going on here 3

CHAPTER

Beyond the frame

The stepping-in technique makes it easier for children to imagine what might exist beyond the frame of the picture. You might simply say, 'I want you to step into the scene and, sitting quietly with your eyes closed if you prefer, have a good look around. Talk to the characters if you like and listen to what they say. In a few minutes you can tell us what you've noticed'.

Set a time limit of a minute or so and instruct the children to step back out when that interval has passed. If you run the activity again, extend the limit by 15 to 30 seconds each time. This practice helps children to turn their attention inward while developing their concentration span and metacognitive skill (the ability to notice and manipulate one's own thoughts).

Take it further:

- A walk around town. Extend the visualisation by suggesting that children explore the neighbourhood beyond the picture. Allow more time for this. Afterwards, children can draw a map of the area or attempt a written description.
- From here to there. This is where children visualise a real journey based on places they know well – visiting every room in their house, the route from home to school, to a friend's house, to the local shops and so on. As a follow-up, ask children to notice a few things they've never noticed before, or forgotten about, when they make the journey again in reality.
- Fantastical adventures. In subsequent visualisations, suggest that the children take a different point of view. They might still 'be themselves', but now they can fly and look down on the town or surrounding area. Or they might imagine themselves as the cat, or a leaf blown by the wind or a bird in a tree, etc.
- Prompted visualisation. This is where you use a light touch to gently guide what you want the children to imagine. Prepare a list of words and as children put themselves in the picture, read out the words one at a time with a 10- to 15-second gap in between. So – car – person – unexpected

event – crowd – funny – chase – object and so on. Each child will interpret these words differently. Invite children to share their visualisations afterwards.

- Guided visualisation. This is a more prescriptive set of instructions that puts greater detail into what you want the children to imagine. It can be used as preparation for writing a story. So, 'As you stand on the street corner, a car pulls up and the driver turns off the engine (notice at least three things about the car). The driver gets out of the car but leaves the door open (notice something interesting or unusual about the driver). The driver then hurries away and vanishes around the corner. Moments later there is the crash of glass and a loud scream (imagine what you think might have happened)'.

Tip: Here is an opportunity to introduce or revisit the second person in writing. The 'you-voice', where the writer speaks to the reader or audience, is relatively little used these days. It is to be found though in a range of popular choose-your-own-adventure books, which first came out in the 1970s and are still available today. It adds immediacy to a narrative by speaking directly to the reader/listener.

Figure 25.1 Cat on the corner 3

An example:

Go down to the end of the road and turn left. What do you notice?

Walk twenty paces. You come across a box. There will be something interesting inside. When you know what it is go to the corner and wait.

Now you become aware of a person not far away speaking into a cell phone. Notice something about the person's appearance or voice that will help you to recognise him/her in the future.

Keep walking until you see a toy shop across the street. It's still open. Cross the road and look through the shop's window. There's something there that you'd really like to have.

Step into the shop. The person at the counter fetches the item from the window, allowing you to examine it in great detail (you can go into kinaesthetic submodalities here: weight, texture, temperature).

Then suddenly something dramatic happens that takes you and the shop assistant by surprise.

And so it goes on. Notice how the visualisation is constructed:

- Short clear instructions.
- Use of artful vagueness.
- 'Sensory neutral' use of 'notice' rather than see or hear, as appropriate.
- Inclusion of stimulus words such as interesting, fascinating, dramatic, unexpected.
- Second person, the 'you' voice.

CHAPTER

Cinematic method of describing a picture

We started exploring the imagination by asking children to 'be nosy' by noticing and asking questions. We hope that having come this far, they will have more mental tools available for drawing further information out of images and for using their imaginations more effectively when reading and writing.

Another technique that might prove useful is the cinematic method of describing a picture. This uses some of the vocabulary of cinematography as guidelines for organising descriptive writing. These include the following:

- Aerial shot. Here children imagine they are floating above the scene, looking down.
- Bridging shot. This indicates a jump in time. In written form, this might simply amount to 'six months went by' for example, though underpinning these words is a leap of the imagination that a child must make – viewing the scene before and after – having decided what interval has passed.
- Camera angle defines the point of view the mind's eye will assume. In a high-angle shot, the camera is higher than the subject, looking down, while in a low-angle shot it is lower, so looking up. (This technique is similar to asking children to imagine a bird's-eye view, a worm's-eye view, a cat's-eye view, etc.)
- Close up. In writing, this is a detailed description of a small area.
- Crosscutting. Jumping between different events in space and/or time. This exercise of the imagination helps children to master writing in the third person.
- Establishing shot. Filmically, this is usually a long shot used to set the scene. In writing, it would amount to one or two sentences that act as a 'doorway' into the story or scene. So for instance, using the following picture (Figure 26.1), an opening might be, 'The weary rider came to the crest of the hill and gazed out over the cloud-covered valley and the mountains beyond'.
- Flashback/flash-forward. A jump in time to the past or the future where a scene is inserted into the present-time sequence of events.

Cinematic method of describing a picture

Figure 26.1 Weary rider

- Foreshadowing. This is not strictly a film-related term, though it links with the idea of a flash-forward. Foreshadowing is an indication of a future event, often used to create a sense of anticipation in the reader.
- Framing. In writing, this is related to the idea of directing the reader's attention towards what you want him or her to imagine. In film it means deciding on the boundaries of what the camera makes visible to the audience.
- Pan. To move the camera to the left or right while filming. In writing, panning left for example would mean describing the weary rider picture from the right-hand side towards the left. The idea can be extended vertically – describing the picture from top to bottom or vice versa, or diagonally from any of the corners. The word 'panning' derives from panorama.
- Point of view shot. Describing the scene from a character's viewpoint (see page 67).
- Zoom in/out. To focus in on smaller details of a scene or to 'draw back' so that a more general view of the scene is revealed. In writing, to achieve this means using the imaginative technique of going beyond the frame (page 72).

CHAPTER

Studying pictures

So far children have been looking at individual pictures. Here are some activities using two or more images, easily accessed online:

- Pick an image and use it in conjunction with the kinds of questions mentioned on page 147. Reframe the questions so that they are closed and as such an answer can be found by flipping a two-colour counter (page 143).
- Select pictures that can be linked by a theme such as 'a journey', 'fear' or 'neighbourhood'.
- Pick an image of a character. Play the counter-flip game to learn more about him or her before 'jumping into' that character. Then:
- Put your character-self into a picture. Why are you there? What are your thoughts and feelings?
- Have a conversation with a friend who is also a character inside the same picture.
- Pick two pictures at random. Imagine one is at the start of a story and the other is at the end. What might happen in between?
- Pick a picture and describe it in a letter or text message to a friend.
- Pick an image that gives you a certain feeling, such as 'uneasy'. Find other pictures that give you the same feeling. If you can, put them in order of – in this case – uneasiness. What clues do you notice in each picture that create the feeling inside you?
- Suggest different titles for some of the pictures.
- If it isn't obvious why a picture has been given a certain title, work with your friends to create a 'group maybe hand' (page 16) of possible explanations.

CHAPTER

Sensory journey

This is an activity combining elements of the jump-in activity with the kind of metacognitive visualisation work described earlier – where one's awareness is more internalised and the conscious point of attention is focussed on the flow of thoughts across the range of sensory domains. The sensory journey also encourages children to think beyond the obvious in writing short vivid descriptions of what they imagine.

Here's what to do:

Decide in advance, at least to some extent, what your sensory journey will be about.

Break the journey down into small bits with a specific 'sensory focus'. The example that follows shows you what we mean.

Pause between each section to give children the chance to jot down their thoughts. Ask for short descriptive sentences or phrases, or even unconnected words – just whatever impressions come to mind. If any child doesn't want to write anything or feels she or he can't, never put pressure on the child to 'try'. The primary value of the activity is the thinking the children do rather than any written outcome that may result.

1. Pretend you own a car and you're old enough to drive. You only had enough money to buy a rather old motor, but usually it runs well. You wake up one sunny Saturday morning and decide to take a trip to the seaside. Your car has been parked outside your apartment all night (you own the apartment too!). You sit in your car and try to start the engine, but it's cold and won't fire up. You try and try by pumping the accelerator pedal – and suddenly you notice a strong smell of petrol in the car. Pretend I have never smelt petrol fumes before. How would you describe them to give me that smell in my nose?

Note: It's important to explain to the children that you're not looking for their opinions of what the fumes smell like. Responses like 'horrible' or 'gross' or 'lovely' won't do. That's what a child might think *about* the fumes rather than trying to convey a direct sensory impression to you the reader/listener.

Also, discourage easy get-outs like 'petrolly' or 'oily'. If a child responds in that way respond by saying, 'But I don't know what a petrolly smell is because I've never smelt petrol or oil before'. As you'll see next, you can challenge other words that also indicate an easy option, often the product of lazy thinking.

Emphasise that the point of the children's description is to create in you a strong impression, in this case of the smell of petrol. You want to experience it as powerfully as possible. Bring it right back to the physiology: by emphasising what would be your physical reaction to smelling the fumes, you're focussing the children's attention on what their own physical reaction would be. This shifts their minds away from struggling to think of words into how petrol fumes *feel* in the nose.

Anyway, on with the journey …

2. Wind the windows down to clear away the fumes and wait for a minute or two before trying again. Although the day is sunny, clouds have been bubbling up and unexpectedly there's a short heavy rain shower. Imagine now that you're sitting listening to the sound of that rain on the roof of the car. And without using words like splish-splash or pitter-patter (wait for the children to stop groaning) or even drumming, describe the sound of that rain so that I can hear it too.

3. After a few minutes the shower passes. You try the ignition key again; the engine fires into life and you enjoy a hassle-free drive to the coast. You park at the top of a ridge of sand dunes and gaze out across the wide flat beach to the sea. The tide's out and the water is a few minutes' walk away. You look in your beach bag for your sandshoes but realise you have forgotten to pack them. So you walk down the dunes barefoot, which is fine.

    Soon, however, you come to a broad strip of shingle. Notice that some of the pebbles are big, some small. Most are rounded but there may be a few fragments with sharper edges. You notice as well that some of the stones are wet and will be cool, while others are dry and will be warm where the sun has shone on them. You have no choice but to walk across the shingly stretch with your bare feet. Go ahead and do it – writing down exactly what it feels like so that I can feel those pebbles under my feet too. (Again, you may want to disallow words like ouch, it's horrible, really hurts, etc.)

4. You soon cross the shingle and walk across the flat sand to the water. The sea is gentle just now – notice how those little waves ripple up over your toes. The water's pleasantly warm too. You walk along the shoreline for a while until the sight and sound of the ocean make you feel thirsty. You look in your beach bag and find a bottle of your favourite drink (whether you ban alcohol is up to you!) Take a good long guzzle of that drink and then describe it so that I can taste it and feel it in my mouth also.

Sensory journey

5. Much refreshed, you walk on. Soon you can see a small group of children up ahead flying kites. You stop and watch them. The kites are different shapes, sizes and colours. A few have fancy tails that twirl about. You can also hear the sound the kites make as they swoop and flutter[1] in the air. Be aware of the whole scene of those children flying kites and write a sentence or some phrases that help me to imagine exactly what you're seeing and hearing.

When we run this particular sensory journey we use the previous five steps and then, depending on the time we have left or the children's inclination to keep going, we'll either make up further steps as we go along or end the activity in the following way:

6. After your walk, you arrive back at the dunes and scramble up towards your car. The slope is quite steep and you have to use your hands to help you climb (notice the weight of your beach bag slung over your back and shoulders). Feel the fine, warm, dry sand under your hands. When you reach the top of the dunes keep a handful of that sand and let it slide between your fingers and tip out of your palm. Notice how that feels and describe it so that I can feel the sand too.
7. As the last of the sand slips away you notice that a little shell is left in the middle of your palm. You realise now that there are probably thousands of shells scattered in the sand, but fate has brought this one to you. Be aware of the shape, the colour, the feel of that shell. Smell it. Blow gently into it and notice the delicate sound you hear. You decide to keep this little shell as a memento of your journey. But before going home, describe that shell so I know exactly what it's like.

The shell serves to sum up the children's experience and to fix it in their minds. From time to time you can remind them of the shell – get them to hold it in their hands and see it in their mind's eye again. In this way it will become a mental anchor for the experience of the whole sensory journey.

Note

1. It's difficult not to put in some descriptive vocabulary yourself as you instruct the class. You can do it deliberately to give the children that need it some words they can copy into their own descriptions, or you might choose to say that these are the kinds of words the children can use but not those specific examples.

CHAPTER

Educational value of the sensory journey

As well as the benefits children gain in terms of developing their metacognitive abilities, the sensory journey activity also has the following value.

- It shows children how ideas can be sequenced and paced. Some children tend to rush through a story, but here you are showing them how to pause, notice details and imagined impressions and take time to find the words that convey those impressions vividly.
- Although a sensory journey is not as tightly 'plotted' as a story would be, it still has a sequence of events, settings, characters and (here in the form of the shell) a 'rounding off' of the adventure. It also needs to have a certain logical consistency. The beach bag was created to carry the bottle of refreshment. The weather conditions were set up to allow a sudden heavy shower to happen. You need to be aware of the logic of the narrative as you create it for the children. Without the beach bag a child might reasonably ask, 'So have I been carrying my bottle of drink all the way from the car?' Such questions interrupt the flow of the activity and can be distracting, especially if you have to think of explanations suddenly off the top of your head. But by giving the logical consistency of the adventure some thought beforehand you can use it as a teaching point for the class.
- You're also demonstrating the fact that short, simple, well-chosen words and phrases can often convey more vivid and powerful impressions than long explanations that 'try and do everything' for the reader. We tell children that a good writer writes *just enough*, and it's the reader's imagination that does much of the work.
- By focussing on the senses and the physiology, you're giving children a robust strategy for 'showing not telling'. Many writers offer the advice show don't tell. 'Show' means to give the reader an emotional/physical experience. Telling is simply putting over an idea in a more abstract or 'intellectual' way.

So if a child writes, 'The man felt frightened as he walked into the haunted house' she's simply telling us that but not creating a direct means for the readers to experience that fear vicariously. There are two things you can say to turn the child's telling into a showing, both of which rely on the useful idea of 'what clues do you notice'.

- Look into your own imagination. What clues do you notice that make you sense that the house is haunted? (Here the child is likely to give you more specific details, such as shadows, strange glows in the window, a door banging – and the obligatory owl hooting in the trees).
- Jump into that mental picture and pretend to be the character. What clues do you notice about him to let you know that he's frightened? (Here the child might talk about the man shivering, his heart beating fast, sweating, feeling tense, etc.).

Once a child has these more specific details in mind she can feed them back into the writing, thus creating a more powerful impression for the reader.

- Children see what value you're putting not only on the careful choice of words but also the time it might take to select them.
- You're implicitly allowing young writers to take ownership of their ideas. This can only happen of course when they are the children's *own* ideas. An idea that is owned allows the creator to have pride in it ('I made this!') and control over what happens to it – if it needs to be changed and how, whether it's used in this piece of work or that.
- Finally, the feedback session where children read out or tell you about what they've written is an ideal opportunity for you to motivate further with sincere praise ('I like what you wrote because...'). It also creates a meaningful context where you can introduce or reinforce the technical aspects of good writing: alliteration and other literary devices, vivid details, strong verbs and adjectives, the composition of sentences and so on.

CHAPTER

Vivid particularities

These are small vivid details that have an impact on both the imagination and the emotions. Sprinkling some into a piece of work (even non-fiction forms such as a reasoned argument or factual essay) helps to bring the writing alive. The techniques that we have looked at so far help children to create vivid particularities more easily, the pupil's 'cloudless in-the-middle-of-nowhere June blue' on page 31 being a good example. Others that have stuck in our minds include the following:

The beggar stooped to pick up an old penny that nobody else had noticed. It was the only shiny thing in his life.

He had kept his head down all his life, but now he looked up and saw the stars for the first time.

The kitten's fur smelled sweet like roses.

He crunched the apple and summerjuice poured into his mouth.

The sound of the gun was like the door of life slamming shut.

Vivid particularities can also establish a clear memory in learners' minds and make an idea or indeed an entire lesson memorable. For instance, Steve still remembers many years after reading a biography of the poet John Keats the occasion where Keats sits up in bed with a racking cough. A moment later he notices a bright spot of blood on his white pillow. Because he was trained as an apothecary, Keats knew that the blood and the cough were symptoms of tuberculosis. Although he travelled to Italy in search of a cure, he found none and died a year later at the age of 26. That image, of the bright blood spot on the white linen, brings extra poignancy to his poem 'When I Have Fears That I May Cease to Be'.

Steve also remembers when, as a student, his biology teacher said that a sea anemone on a rock when the tide is out looks like 'a half-sucked wine gum'. Those exact words have stuck in his mind all these years when so much else of the course has been forgotten.

We're not suggesting that you build such graphic images into all of your lessons, though it's well established that learning happens most effectively with an emotional underpinning. But it may be that finding a powerful image or relevant anecdote to humanise the knowledge will not only engage the children's interest more but also help them to remember the topic far longer. For instance, we remember a Year 6 lesson about the solar system. The teacher was talking about Mars and mentioned that when the famous astronomer and writer Carl Sagan was a child, he became fascinated by the brightness and redness of the planet, such that he really wanted to go there. He would stand under the starry skies out back of his house staring at Mars and then raise his arms and wish with all his heart that he could travel there. Wishing didn't make it happen, though it did inspire Sagan and shape his future career, which included close involvement with NASA's plans to send unmanned probes to Mars and beyond.

Apropos Sagan's interest in Mars, in 1971 he was part of a panel discussion that included the science fiction writers and visionaries Ray Bradbury and Arthur C. Clarke. The topic was 'Mars and the Mind of Man'. The panel took place on November 12, the day before NASA's Mariner 9 mission reached Mars and became the first spacecraft to orbit another planet. The discussion ranged far into the future and how human beings might reach the Red Planet, live on it and use it as a stepping stone to venture even farther into space.

We mention this to highlight the fact that the vision must come before the achievement.

For more on this, follow the www.brainpickings.org link.

There is no simple formula for the creation of vivid particularities, but they are more likely to appear when you encourage your groups to

- notice small details,
- look for new links between ideas,
- go beyond the obvious and immediate when using similes and metaphors,
- play with words in the ways we've been exploring and
- notice the impact of other people's writing.

Instructional writing. Combine a list of instructions with extended visualisations, as in Tyler's experience on page 46. If you write them yourself beforehand, you can introduce vocabulary that you want the children to learn. If your visualisation is genre based, bring some of the motifs and conventions of your chosen genre into the activity. You can also incorporate places, characters and events drawn from stories you are reading with the class. Suggesting that children might have ideas for stories of their own as they experience the visualisation might indeed lead to that very outcome. If your visualisation is more story-like rather than a descriptive exploration (as in 'A Walk Around Town'), then consider ending with a cliffhanger and invite the children to imagine how the plot will unfold and resolve.

Once children have had some practice at guided visualisations, they can create their own to share with classmates, making them up as noted earlier or based on stories they've already written or read. Doing this helps children to realise that an important component of writing fiction is directing the reader's attention. In guided visualisations you are focussing the children's attention on certain objects and events, yet there is a degree of artful vagueness (page 57) in what you say, allowing creative space for a range of possible interpretations. So for instance you instructed children to notice 'something interesting or unusual' about the driver in the example on page 86: it's likely that each child will notice something different. Sharing these various impressions creates a resource bank of descriptive details that children can use in future pieces of work. Incidentally, if any child notices something that's highly unlikely or silly or inappropriate, point out that the idea is only acceptable if it's based on a sound reason that improves the story. So if a child reports that the driver is ten feet tall, ask how that fact might help the story to work (you might also point out that such a tall person would not be able to fit in the car).

Finished stories might be thought of as 'scripted visualisations', where the reader's or listener's attention is fully directed throughout. An important aspect of writing fiction, and standard advice for aspiring writers, is show don't tell. In other words, as writers we try to allow readers to experience the story through describing actions, conveying the characters' thoughts and feelings, using multisensory references and vivid details. So we could say that the driver was frightened, which is just telling, or describe the frightened look in his eyes, the sheen of sweat on his brow, the way his hand trembled as he opened the door and so on.

- And then? The previous guided visualisation suggests a story. Ask children to imagine that it happens at the beginning of the tale and then discuss what might happen next. You can use the 'maybe hand' technique (page 16) to encourage groups to come up with multiple possible storylines.
- Noticing the details. Offer the class a sentence such as, 'The stranger walked hurriedly down the street'. In order to 'process' the words, children will need to visualise the scene. It's likely that many will have put more detail into their mental scenario than the words themselves describe. Ask children to go back to the scenario in their imaginations and note down some of these extra details.

CHAPTER

Creative conversations

An extension of the visualisation activity in the previous section is to organise the class into pairs. Give each pair a starter sentence like the 'The stranger walked hurriedly down the street'. One child will act as the questioner and the other will be the one doing the visualising. Demonstrate this first by asking for a volunteer to do the visualising while you ask the questions. The numbers in the following example refer to points of commentary.

You: 'The stranger walked hurriedly down the street'. Tell me when you've noticed (1) that (child nods a moment later). Tell me two or three interesting things about the stranger (2).

Child: He's wearing a pale trench coat and a hat pulled down so that you can't see his eyes. His shoes are black and polished.

Y: So it's definitely a man?

C: Yes, I just know it is.

Y: Decide if this scene is set in modern times or in the past and tell me when (3) you know.

C: It's modern times.

Y: OK. Is the scene based on the cat on the corner picture we looked at earlier? (4)

C: No, although the man is walking down an empty street, and it is night. The pavement is wet because it's been raining. But it's a different street to the one in the cat picture.

Y: Now the man stops. He takes out his mobile and makes a call. You can hear him. Tell me something about (5) the tone of his voice. (6)

C: He's speaking quickly, and he sounds panicky. He's in some kind of danger.

Y: Before he finishes the call, a car appears at the end of the street. It screams around the corner, its tyres screeching on the wet road. (7) It accelerates towards him.

C: The street is a pedestrian area...

Y: OK, so how about the car screeches to a halt? The doors fly open, and four shady figures scramble out and run towards him. (8)

C: All right.

Y: Notice the one who seems to be in charge and tell me something interesting about that person...

With a little practice most children can concentrate and systematically daydream in this way (as opposed to idly daydreaming) for quite long periods of time. If you were running this as a demonstration, then most likely all of the other children in the class would be experiencing their own versions of the scenario. If you then split the class into pairs you might suggest that they carry on with the story, each child taking it in turns to visualise the next part of the narrative, building on the ideas of their partner.

While the exchanges between the children form the primary outcome of the activity because it develops their ability to imagine, further oral, written and/or drawn outcomes can follow.

Setting up creative conversations like this is an effective way of helping children to think their way through a storyline. One reason is that it embodies the principle of flexibility within a structure: the notion of 'systematic' daydreaming implies a definite process for thinking – a how-to technique that children can use subsequently. At the same time, they can enjoy a sense of ownership at having and expressing their own ideas.

Points to note:

1. 'Tell me when you've noticed'. The 'when' here is a presupposition of success, as on page 27.
2. 'Tell me two or three interesting things about the stranger'. Here you're prompting the child to have more than one idea. Also, the word 'stranger' is gender-neutral, allowing the 'imagineer' to decide that in this case, it's a man.
3. 'Decide if this scene is set in modern times or in the past'. Because the questioner is also running the scenario through in her own mind, it's easy to pick elements of what *she's* thinking about, which might clash with what the partner is imagining. Advise children to take care therefore not to make assumptions or jump to conclusions – check to find out what the partner is thinking about before moving on.
4. 'Is the scene based on the cat on the corner picture?' This is a further example of checking. If yes then the questioner and partner immediately have access

to lots of information based on previous work with that picture immediately available. If no, then ask for more details.

5/6. 'Tell me something about the tone of his voice'. 'Something about' is artfully vague (page 57), while asking about the tone of voice prompts the child to begin or continue thinking across more than one sensory domain.

7. 'The car screams around the corner, its tyres screeching on the wet road'. Here the questioner is building on the partner's ideas, based on earlier feedback.

8. As far as possible advise the questioner to accommodate the partner's ideas and try not to impose her own thoughts. Because the partner imagined a pedestrianised area, the questioner needed to think on her feet to tweak the prompt to fit in with the evolving scenario.

- Bare-bones writing. Another way of helping children to develop their ability to visualise is to offer them a sequence of loosely linked statements that suggest a storyline but which are not too prescriptive: this activity is similar to a prompted visualisation (page 72) but not identical to it. Each statement comes with a 'thinking instruction', so allow some time for children to carry this out before moving on to the next. Subsequently, children can write their own sequences. The 'bare-bones' tag means that this activity is a version of the minimal writing ploy we mentioned on page 57. Because (apparently) not much work is involved, less enthusiastic writers are more tempted to join in. In any case, running a bare-bones session instead of asking children to prepare and write a full story can be a refreshing change. Having said that, the session can be used as a precursor to more extended writing.

A widely recognised model for the process of creative thinking postulates four stages: preparation, incubation, illumination and implementation.

Preparation amounts to all the work you do with children in strengthening their imaginations, plus offering them specific information – for instance in a sequence of bare-bones writing statements. In other areas of study such as science, history or whatever, it amounts to the years of learning and experience that underpin new discoveries and insights, so allowing that area of human endeavour to evolve. As Louis Pasteur said, 'Chance favours the prepared mind'.

Incubation. Although children can be thinking consciously about a storyline, a lot of subconscious processing is going on as well. The familiar idea of sleeping on a problem is one example of this. More commonly, many authors have the experience of ideas 'popping into mind' when they have not been consciously thinking about them. These sudden spontaneous insights represent the moment of illumination. Illumination is when an insight becomes conscious; the famous Eureka! moment. It is the result of the subconscious work that preceded it and is symbolised by the image of the lightbulb going on above someone's head.

Implementation (also known as verification) is where the insight is tested in the 'real world' – i.e. when the prototype of a new invention is built or when the story is written – to see if it works.

The information contained in a bare-bones session therefore can be incubated/assimilated at a nonconscious level, leading to a way forward later. We feel that it's worth experimenting with the technique as an alternative to the fully conscious story planning that is usually practised in the classroom.

Here's what a bare-bones sequence might look like:

A boy was walking through the forest.
It was late afternoon.
He needed to reach the village.
He heard a voice calling.
He went to investigate.
The light was fading.
He thought he saw a shadowy figure up ahead.
He walked deeper among the trees.
He felt nervous but curious.
He came to a small house in a clearing.
He went inside.

If the children are creating these statements for themselves, ask them to write on a large sheet of paper. You can prompt them by asking them where the character was, what time of the day or night, what was the character doing, what happens next etc. Note that children don't have to know in any more detail than this regarding what the story will be about. Make sure the children leave large gaps between the statements. Once they have this skeleton of a plot the task is to concentrate on one statement at a time and fill in more details, writing these as notes – not the story itself – around the statement they're thinking about. So if a child was concentrating on 'the boy was walking through the forest', he might add a few details about the boy's appearance, how he was feeling, what the forest looked like (including colours, sounds, smells, etc.).

The statements don't have to be dealt with in order. It might be that the young writer now has some thoughts about the small house in the clearing, so could jump to that sentence next. Nor do children need to make all their notes on any given statement in one sitting. In fact there's a positive benefit in having children come back to the task after a lapse of time, the next day say; the interim counts as potentially fruitful thinking (incubation) time; also, children might notice things that evening or coming to school next morning that they can use to add to what's already on the sheet. This is an interesting phenomenon familiar to many creative people, where things that are seen and heard are uncannily appropriate in the context of the project being developed. This isn't mere coincidence: psychologically, the story or whatever being mulled over acts as a 'perceptual filter', attuning one's awareness to what's 'out there' that may be of use.

Bare-bones writing is an example of the minimal writing strategy, where tasks require relatively little actual writing but lots of thinking, and it is based on the principle that what matters is quality not quantity. Any technique that satisfies those requirements stands more of a chance of attracting so-called reluctant writers. Minimal writing tasks combined with techniques that show children how to generate and organise their ideas are usually very motivating.

Tip: Consider using the principle of minimal writing when you want children to correct or redraft their work. Why not ask them just to redraft one scene or even just one paragraph? And instead of telling them to do all of their corrections, suggest that they review the work and make just one or two changes that you and/or they feel improves the work. Similarly, you can mark their work selectively by focussing say only on spellings or strong verbs or some other aspect of the work. This saves you time and means that children aren't overwhelmed by a cascade of corrective marks. As such, it means that they're more likely to take note of your advice.

CHAPTER 32

Imagining impossible things

One of the astonishing powers of the human mind is its ability to imagine people, objects, places and times that might have nothing to do with our present circumstances. By an act of will, we can, as the Red Queen famously said, imagine six impossible things before breakfast – or more, and at any time. Doing so is not merely frivolous or an addictive pastime of fiction writers. Our ability to plan ahead means that we need to extrapolate from our previous experiences in order to envision a future that does not yet exist, projecting our thoughts forward in time to conceive of possible scenarios so that we can prepare as necessary for these. To some extent in doing this we are predicting what is more or less likely to occur. When someone does this on a grander scale, based on wide experience and with wisdom, that person is called a visionary. An online search will quickly throw up a host of names from various branches of human endeavour: business, politics, technology and science. We were ourselves inspired by the writings of Arthur C. Clarke as well as by his galaxy-spanning and hugely optimistic visions of human expansion across the universe. See, for instance, Clarke (1999a, 1999b).

Steve's love of Clarke's science fiction stories (as well as the earliest Doctor Who stories) led both to an interest in 'real' science and in writing, which by his mid-teens had transformed the course of his life and given him a deep and ongoing sense of purpose.

Acts of imagination also feature in science and other areas of knowledge in the form of thought experiments. These often stem from asking a what-if question within a particular field of enquiry. (The author Douglas Hill felt that all science fiction began by asking 'what if?') Albert Einstein for example when he was only 16, began wondering what would happen if you could chase a beam of light as it travelled through space (at around 186,000 miles per second). If this were possible, then you would see the light frozen in space – which would be scientifically impossible, as it wouldn't then be light. Following this train of thought helped Einstein to formulate his groundbreaking special and general theories of relativity.

Another scientist, the German chemist August Kekulé, achieved a different kind of breakthrough in the research he was doing on a class of chemicals known as benzenes. Two vital insights came in the form of dreams (or perhaps as what is known as hypnagogic imagery: visions experienced on the threshold of consciousness rather than images recalled after sleep). In the first 'dream', Kekulé saw atoms dancing and linking up with each other. Later, the chains of atoms began to move in a snakelike fashion, coming to resemble snakes more vividly until one serpent curled round and put its tail into its mouth. This led Kekulé to the certain knowledge that the benzene molecule is ringlike. Indeed, it is now called the benzene ring.

It has to be said that Kekulé's insight didn't simply happen. He had been working in the field for years and so had assimilated the great amount of information necessary to allow his mind to produce the dream of snakes and to realise its significance. Kekulé urged his colleagues thus: 'Let us learn to dream, gentlemen, then perhaps we shall find the truth'.

(In the interests of accuracy we must mention that the German chemist Joseph Loschmidt proposed a cyclic arrangement of six carbon atoms for the benzene ring in 1861, five years before Kekulé – www.britannica.com.)

CHAPTER

More thought experiments

According to the plato.stanford.edu website, thought experiments should contain something 'experimental' about them, which is to say they should not be visualisations of a counterfactual or hypothetical nature – i.e. not imagining experiments that could never be carried out in the 'real world' now or at some point in the future (though Einstein broke the rule and that led him to real-world discoveries). That said, helping children to imagine impossible things such as turning a tennis ball inside out without cutting into it or a battle between a dragon and a unicorn, helps to build the mental flexibility necessary to carry out the kind of thought experiment more rigorously defined earlier. It must also be said that thought experiments like Albert Einstein's were only possible because of the vast amount of knowledge and experience he had in his field. Similarly with August Kekulé's insight – though here the eureka moment occurred when a huge amount of subconscious work led to the intuition popping into consciousness.

An effective way of explaining thought experiments to children is to liken them to what-if adventures or scenarios. In the philosophy of ethics for example one of the most famous thought experiments is known as the trolley problem. So what if you came upon the situation where a number of strangers were lying injured across a nearby railway track. An unmanned trolley car is hurtling down the hill towards them. You find yourself standing close to a lever that controls a switch that can change the points and divert the trolley along a branch line before it reaches the injured people. However, as you move to do this you see that your friend, also injured, is lying unconscious across the branch line tracks. You do not have time to reach your friend or any of the strangers to drag them free. What do you decide to do?

Incidentally, in some analyses of the trolley problem doing nothing also counts as a decision.

Although such a situation could occur in reality, essentially the experiment's purpose is to focus reflection on one's own values, beliefs and motivations.

You can take this kind of visualisation further by inventing other scenarios that explore children's moral values more deeply:

- What if you came upon an envelope full of money in the street? There is no one around to see you pick it up. Then you duck into an alley to count the money and find it amounts to £500. What do you do next?

Once children have offered their ideas, test them further:
What if an address was written on the envelope?
What if the money was in a wallet: there's no address but there is a photograph of an elderly person? What if the photograph was of a disabled person? What if the photograph was of a cute kitten? What if the picture showed a snake?
What if the photograph was of a local businessperson that you recognise? What if you know this person is very charitable? What if you know this person is mean and does not treat his or her workers very well?
Continue the activity by increasing the amount of money in the wallet. Also, ask children to imagine that they (or an imagined character) keep the money. Now ask them to come up with reasons to justify that decision – you can also apply the strength of reasons test to explore the children's responses (page 16).

- What if you bought a down-and-out wizard a coffee out of kindness, and afterwards he offered you the chance to live ten healthy years longer than you would do otherwise? However, somewhere in the world someone you'll never meet will have *their* life shortened by ten years. Would you accept the wizard's offer?
- What if, during an important test, you noticed your best friend cheating? Would you tell your teacher? What if, knowing that you will do badly in the test, your friend offered to share his or her answers, thus giving you a great mark?
- What if you could drop two metal balls from a high tower? One ball is light and the other is heavy. Which one would reach the ground first? Why do you think this?

Note: This experiment is called 'Galileo's balls'. You might not want to tell the children that, but if you type it into a search engine, you'll come up with more information about it, including video demonstrations. Aristotle believed that heavier objects fall faster than lighter ones under the influence of gravity. But consider this extension to the thought experiment – suppose the two balls were tied together. Is it the case that the lighter ball will therefore slow the heavier one so that the heavier ball would take longer to reach the ground than if it fell singly? But then the two balls tied together weigh more than the heavier one alone, so isn't it the case that they'd reach the ground more quickly than the heavier ball falling alone?

It's not known whether Galileo actually dropped balls from a tower (supposedly the leaning tower of Pisa), but by carrying out the thought experiment he realised that acceleration due to gravity doesn't depend upon the mass of an object. This was demonstrated dramatically during the Apollo 15 lunar mission in 1971 when Commander David Scott dropped a geologic hammer and a feather from the same height. They both hit the lunar surface together (again, video clips can be found online).

- Imagine that everyone in the class is given a box with the word 'beetle' written on it. Because of this, everyone calls what's in the box a beetle. However, none of the children is allowed to describe what's in their box, nor can they show it to anyone. So it's possible that every child has something different in the box or maybe nothing at all.

The point of this thought experiment is to highlight the idea that what we experience may not be the same as what *you* experience. Does the colour blue for instance look the same to all of us? How could we ever prove it? This has both scientific and philosophical implications: if you wanted to delve a little deeper try Law's (2002), Chapter 4, 'What's Real?' and Thomas Nagel's 'What Does It All Mean?' (Nagel (1997)), especially Chapter 2 'How Do We Know Anything?' and Chapter 3 'Other Minds'.

- Would-you-rather. This game is similar to some of the thought experiments we've already mentioned. Children are asked to decide between two real or hypothetical options, giving reasons as necessary.

> Would you rather be able to walk through solid objects or fly?
> Would you rather travel to a past or a future time of your choice?
> Would you rather be cleverer or more popular?
> Would you rather be a favourite fictional character or a real person of your choice?
> Would you rather be a superhero in a virtual world for the rest of your life or yourself as you are in the real world?

Tip: If you put 'would you rather game for kids' into your search engine you'll find many more examples.

- Paradox. Thought experiments can also be used to introduce the idea of paradox. This is a statement or scenario that proceeds from valid or reasonable premises but which entails apparently insoluble contradictions. The best known is perhaps, what came first, the chicken or the egg? Use this as a mind warm-up before going on to the following more elaborate examples.
- The Ship of Theseus is a famous philosophical paradox. Imagine that the Greek hero Theseus possessed a fine ship that took him on many exciting adventures. Every now and then he would need to instruct his crew to replace a part that

was wearing out. After 40 years every single part of the ship had been replaced. Is it still the same ship?

This paradox focusses on the concept of identity. Similarly (although according to livescience.com it's a myth), all the cells in the human body have been replaced after a seven- or ten-year period. If that's true, are you the same person you were seven/ten years ago? Common sense says yes, but what aspect of yourself are you referring to if you decide you are the same person now as then?

- The omnipotence paradox. Imagine a being that is all-powerful (there is no need to call it God). Could such a being create a rock too heavy for him/her/it to lift? Could the same being create a square circle? Are these questions valid, and if not why not?

These notions often crop up in theological discussions about whether God (or the Ultimate Being, etc.) exists or not and frequently accompany the famous 'problem of evil': if God is all-loving as well as all-powerful, how come 'bad things happen to good people'? If you're interested in this debate, try the closertotruth.com website.

- The time traveller. A scientist invents a time machine. She travels back 50 years but accidentally lands on her maternal grandfather, killing him before he ever marries. So in that case the time traveller never existed to build the time machine that killed her grandfather. Therefore, the grandfather wasn't squashed by a time machine: he lived to marry and he and his wife produced the girl who was to become the time traveller's mother.

One ingenious 'solution' to this paradox is the suggestion that at the moment of the grandfather's death, another timeline is created. On one time track the grandfather dies, while on the other one he doesn't. The time traveller returns to a future (her present) where she did not kill her grandfather. Of course, you can explore the idea further by positing that the time traveller goes back into the past again and, oh no, squashes her grandfather. To resolve the paradox, is yet another timeline created?

Science more broadly relies on the ability to envision a bigger and richer picture based on inference and extrapolation from limited data. Most if not all children are familiar with the world of the dinosaurs, yet the rich landscapes and diverse range of creatures we see in books and films needed to be imagined in the first place based on fossil evidence. This is an obvious point to make, but its importance needs to be highlighted: that imagination gives information vitality, colour, life and immediacy. John Habgood in 'Varieties of Unbelief' (Habgood (2000), P18) points out that the creation of the world of the dinosaurs in our imaginations opens up our 'time horizons', allowing us to comprehend and wonder about the great vistas of time separating us from the Jurassic and Cretaceous eras – the temporal equivalent of the notion that travel broadens the mind.

Habgood also makes the point (P23), echoing Wittgenstein, that the limits of our language mark the limits of our world. Imagining prehistory for example relies on our ability to articulate our ideas, firstly to ourselves and then to others, which in turn requires a rich language 'full of overtones and associations capable of disclosing or hinting at what lies beyond the reach of inventiveness and insight'.

For more mind-bending ideas, see Cohen (2003); Stock (2004); William (2015).

CHAPTER

Inspiration

Acts of imagination can also inspire as well as offer insights and ways forward. It might just take one book, poem, film or piece of music to stir our hearts as well as our minds, sometimes creating a desire or an energy so intense that it changes one's entire life.

- Ask children what they think the word 'inspiration' means. (We've found that children can be wonderfully perceptive in answering this question.)
- Follow up by asking if children can bring to mind an image or memory of something that actually happened, or from the world of fiction, that they found to be inspirational.
- On a different occasion, ask the children to visualise the following. Only do a couple at a time.

Imagine a tree going through its entire life cycle in 30 seconds.

Imagine you are the world's number one at any sport of your choice (even if you're not particularly interested in that sport). Or, if sport doesn't appeal at all, pick some other activity or profession.

Imagine you were alive at some period in history that you've studied. Remember to use all five senses, plus your feelings.

Create a vision of what you think the world might be like in 50 years' time.

Imagine that you are taking a trip through your own body. Use whatever knowledge you have to help with this, but feel free to make up your own impressions. For instance, you may not know what the inside of your lungs looks like but use the fact that you know that lungs are used for breathing to create a picture.

Imagine that dinosaurs lived again (as in the Jurassic Park films) and that you could travel to see them.

Imagine you are an animal. Decide which and take a 'day in the life of' journey.

Apropos this last example, the modern philosopher Thomas Nagel wondered what it would be like to be a bat so that he could think further about the mind-body problem in philosophy. Briefly, this concerns the relationship between human consciousness/the mind and its relationship to the brain/body. There are many possible responses to the issue but as yet no definitive answer or any significant degree of consensus. There's plenty of information online and Stephen Law's *Philosophy Files* is useful if you wanted to discuss the issue with the children.

CHAPTER

A medley of visualisations

Here are some prompted and guided visualisations, taken from different genres, to try with the class. They can be used purely to help children develop their imaginations but also serve as guides for plotting storylines, as story openers or as the basis for descriptive writing. Prompted visualisations are lists of loosely connected words: guided visualisations are more detailed and prescriptive.

Tip: If used for plotting, children can write their ideas on sticky notes and arrange them along a narrative line. If this is drawn on a large sheet of paper there will be plenty of room to add further details, which might be rearranged as the plan develops. The example is based on the prompted fantasy visualisation that follows (Figure 35.1).

When using the prompted visualisations, leave about 10 or 15 seconds between each word.
Take it further:

- Invite children to write their own prompted visualisations. A variation of this is the 'chain visualisation'. Here, one child writes the first word and then passes

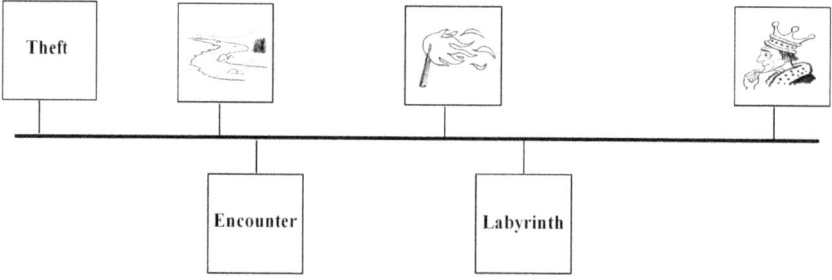

Figure 35.1 Storyline

the sheet on to her neighbour, who writes the second, etc. Several visualisations can be doing the rounds simultaneously. Make sure that characters, places and objects are included. Note also that some of the words are artfully vague, as in the fantasy example; 'theft' and 'encounter' suggest events but leave a creative space that allows for various interpretations.

Both prompted and guided visualisations can also act as the focus for discussing parts of speech. Abstract nouns, strong adjectives and verbs work well. Combine this with asking the children what kinds of things make for an exciting story – a chase, a fight, action, thrills, etc.

In guided visualisations, children can become characters in the story. Let them think about this beforehand: whether they will be themselves or, if not, what the new persona will be like in terms of physical appearance and personality.

Tip: If children imagine themselves as another character, ask them to visualise looking at their other-self in a mirror.

Tip: Rearranging the words in prompted visualisations creates different plot lines.

Fantasy

Theft – river – encounter – fire – labyrinth – king

You are walking along a forest path. It's autumn. Notice the colours of the leaves, the sound of the breeze in the tree canopy, the smell of damp earth and the coolness of the air. (Pause.) You hear the sound of a horse galloping some distance ahead. You have been warned that this is dangerous territory and consider hiding until the rider passes by. Before you decide, someone bursts out of the undergrowth and runs towards you. Notice this person in detail. (Pause.) 'The Revenger is coming – can't you hear? We must run. Follow me. I know a safe place'. The stranger points to a barely visible path between the trees. You wonder whether this person can be trusted.

Tip: After each guided visualisation allow the children some more thinking time to continue imagining the story if they wish.

Pirate adventure

Island – ship – storm – map – beach – attack – find – meeting

You are walking through foggy city streets at night. The year is 1786. Times have been difficult lately. (Pause.) As you turn a corner you see a man being set upon by thieves. You rush to help. After a scuffle, you and the victim drive the attackers away.

The person you helped is very grateful and offers you the chance to join a ship's crew, which would mean a life of adventure but also danger. You think carefully about the opportunity, and then...

Ghost Story

Country road – mystery – diversion – shadow – meeting – destination

Now you realise that you and your friend were foolish to accept the dare. The place seemed innocent enough when you first got there. (Pause.) Now though you are both having doubts. The light is failing and you begin to feel uneasy as you both realise you don't know how to find your way back. Your surroundings look strange, eerie. (Pause.) Up ahead you hear the sound of someone sighing.

Thriller

Pursuit – meeting – exchange – travel – danger – agreement – betrayal – escape

You can hear the echoing cries of the prisoner coming from the floor below. You hurry down the spiral staircase and run along the corridor until you come to the wooden door of the cell. You place a small explosive device on the lock. (Pause.) After it detonates you kick the door open and rush forward to help the prisoner stand. (Pause.) As you leave the room an alarm sounds and you hear guards shouting. Your only safe route is upwards onto the roof. You hope your partner got your message and will arrive in time by helicopter.

CHAPTER

Reframing

In the context of writing stories, this technique tempts the reader or viewer to predict a certain outcome but then reveals an unexpected conclusion. See the visual example in Figure 36.1.

Sometimes children's stories are predictable, but by encouraging them to think of alternative and unexpected scenes, chapters or whole-story endings, the work can be more enjoyable both to read and to write.

Reframing is also a psychological technique to improve mental and emotional wellbeing. Transactional analysis theory posits that our behaviour is influenced by 'life scripts', patterns of thinking and feeling laid down in childhood, often as the result of explicit or implicit 'messages' that we pick up from adult authority figures. Life scripts can of course be very positive and beneficial, but negative life scripts may well restrict us and limit our potential.

Psychotherapist Kim Schneiderman in her book *Step Out of Your Story: Writing Exercises to Reframe and Transform Your Life* (Schneiderman (2015)) suggests looking at patterns of behaviour as stories, with ourselves as the protagonist/hero. She then advises that we identify a problem in our lives and regard that as the villain, whose power can be diminished when we use our strengths against it. Even stories that are fantastical help to bring strengths and noble qualities to the fore, giving us a fresh perspective on troublesome issues which in effect reframes them.

For instance, during a workshop that Steve was running, one boy, Oliver, began writing a thriller story where the hero – himself – was driving along in a Mini when he spotted a juggernaut in his rear-view mirror coming up quickly.

'Then I went faster'. Oliver said once Steve had read up to that point, 'but the big lorry just keeps getting nearer and nearer. I'm frightened and decide to pull in at the motorway services...'

Oliver wasn't writing now but talking the story through, significantly in the first person and present tense.

'I stop the car and get out and face the juggernaut. The driver gets out too, and I realise that he's no bigger than I am, just some ordinary person'.

DOI: 10.4324/9781003184003-36

Reframing

Figure 36.1 All will be revealed

Oliver got back to his writing and told Steve later that he enjoyed creating the story and felt 'better' after it. His teacher mentioned later that Oliver had been bullied when he was younger, causing him to be anxious: she felt though that 'writing it out has done him some good'.

It's beyond the scope of this book to go into detail about how creating stories can reframe thoughts, feelings and beliefs. To learn more, we recommend Schneiderman's book and Rowshan (1997); Sunderland (2000); Wallas (1985).

CHAPTER

Scrambletales

In Figure 37.1, we see a set of pictures but with the images out of sequence. Make copies, give them out to groups and then ask the children to cut them out and rearrange them in the correct sequence. Ask groups to report back, telling the story or extracting and explaining their reasoning in sequencing the pictures as they did.

Ralph saves Bertha (Figure 37.2)

Show the children the visual and ask them to write out the number sequence that puts the pictures in the right order. The correct sequence is 4 – 6 – 8 – 7 – 2 – 1 – 3 – 5.

To make the task easier, you can read out these captions, which will help any groups that are having difficulty.

1. Ralph is a young puppy whose owners are always telling him off for barking too loudly, but he does this because he's so excited – by everything. 'Remember Ralph, when you go out into the back garden, be as quiet as you can'.
2. Ralph rushes out into the back garden. He sees a bird flying by and barks at it, trying to make friends. 'Quiet, Ralph! You're disturbing the neighbours'.
3. He sees a butterfly going by and barks at it. 'Quiet, Ralph, you're making too much noise!'
4. Ralph sees a cat scuttling along the fence and runs after it, barking louder than ever. 'Ralph, if you carry on we'll have to take you back in!'
5. The cat jumps down into next door's garden. Ralph goes quiet because he can hear the neighbours talking: 'Have you seen Bertha? I've looked everywhere for her. She can't have escaped – I've plugged every hole in the garden!'
6. Ralph listens carefully. He can hear faint scrabbling. He starts barking as loudly as he can. 'Ralph, that's enough. Come on, you're going back in the house'.

Figure 37.1 Scrambletales

Figure 37.2 Ralph saves Bertha

Copyright material from Steve Bowkett and Tony Hitchman (2022), *Visualising Literacy and How to Teach It*, Routledge

7. The neighbours, drawn by Ralph's barking, look between a tree and the fence and find Bertha, their tortoise, wedged there. One of the neighbours calls out, 'Thank you Ralph. We might never have found her otherwise!'
8. The neighbours, taking Bertha with them, go round to Ralph's owners to thank them and make a fuss of him. Ralph, with a big doggy smile, gives a big 'Ralph!' of pleasure.

Ask what clues children looked for in the pictures to create their sequence.

By the way, this story is based on true events. Ralph is so-called because as a puppy his bark actually sounded like 'Ralph!'

Take it further:

- If you enlarge the separate images and laminate them, although this takes some time and effort, you will have a permanent resource that can be used with other groups.
- Leave out one or two pictures in a set and substitute blank sheets. Ask the children to work out what images should appear on the blanks.
- Leave out the final image in each set and invite groups to decide how the story should end. Encourage more than one answer (see the 'maybe hand' page 16).
- Increase the challenge by giving a group two or more sets of out-of-sequence images. Children now have to separate the different stories/extracts and put each set of pictures in the right order.

Tip: Comics are a great resource for scrambletale activities, which children can create to try out with their classmates.

CHAPTER

Linking game

- Invite children to pick two images from the selection (Figure 38.1). If both images were to be used in a story, what would the story be about? Challenge children to tell you in one sentence if they can: the result is a 'seed idea' that can be left alone to assimilate subconsciously (page 88). Subsequently, ask children what else they could include in the narrative – ideas will probably pop into mind effortlessly.
- Once a child has selected two images, ask him or her to visualise these as solid objects. Ask about shape, colour, texture, weight, any sound the objects make, etc.
- Take it further by asking volunteers to select three objects to include in a story. What would the story basically be about? Allow a couple of sentences for the explanation. Each time you repeat the activity, increase the number of objects (though you may find that children do this anyway, trying to out-compete each other).
- Give out a sheet of paper to each child and ask him or her to draw a simple single image. Collect these in. For each pass, pick two images at random for children to link.
- Pick an object and locate it in a more general category. So gun becomes weapon. Another generalisation might be violence or crime. Money becomes wealth and then perhaps security or greed. This activity is a useful way of creating themes that serve as the basis for generating questions to prepare for a philosophical enquiry (see, for example, Buckley (2011); Bowkett (2018)) or as the basis for writing stories and poems.

Check back:

Re-read a short story or an extract to the class. The children will now be more
   experienced in visualising and ought to be able to give you more details when
   you ask them what's in their mind's eye.

Figure 38.1 Linking game

Copyright material from Steve Bowkett and Tony Hitchman (2022), *Visualising Literacy and How to Teach It*, Routledge

CHAPTER

Descriptive writing

We've seen through techniques like 'bare-bones writing' (page 89) and 'creative conversation' (page 86) that when we read or listen to a sentence, our imaginations create many more details than the words themselves convey. This mental ability can be enhanced further by practice in noticing our own thoughts and multisensory thinking.

In this section the focus will be on descriptive writing. Descriptions are obviously a component of narrative writing, where a story is told through a series of events and from one or more points of view. However, descriptive writing per se amounts to 'word pictures' that ideally should trigger vivid details in the reader's mind and deliver some emotional impact.

- Concrete language. Concrete language strengthens descriptive passages by appealing directly to the reader's five senses, in contrast to abstract language, which is woolly and vague. (Though we've seen how the use of artful vagueness – page 57 – allows for some 'creative space' when imagining mental scenarios.)

'It was a pleasant day' is rather abstract, offering the reader almost nothing on which to build a mental picture. Notice also that 'pleasant' is a value judgement that assumes shared experience. Most of us might interpret this as meaning a warm and sunny day, though for someone with sensitivity to sunlight or with agoraphobia, being outside on such a day could be anything but pleasant.

Ask the children now to apply the five senses technique to the idea of a pleasant day to come up with a list of details that could be included in a descriptive paragraph. So for instance

> A blue sky with some light clouds
> A warm and gentle breeze
> The wind whispering through the grass and trees

Descriptive writing

The smell of flowers
The sound of birdsong and the trickling of water from a nearby stream

Notice that none of the details includes the writer's opinion.

Repeat the five senses/neutral details process with one or more of these abstract descriptions to create a paragraph using concrete language:

An old book
Someone's front room
A clear night sky
A funfair
A waterfall

Ask children to write a second draft from the point of view of someone who likes the object, place or experience. Opinions and value judgements can now be included.

Finally, ask children to pick one of these or another example that appeals to them and write a description from the point of view of someone who *doesn't* like the object or place or experience.

This activity can serve as a precursor to sharpening children's debating skills. A useful technique in preparing for a debate is to list points that are in opposition to one's own viewpoint. This helps children to anticipate what others might say and have counterarguments ready.

- Subtle differences. Another element of effective descriptive writing is the ability to 'tease out' subtle differences between similar objects, experiences, etc. You can approach this activity by focussing on one sense at a time. So in terms of taste for example, how would you explain the difference between the taste of white chocolate, milk chocolate and dark chocolate? For smell, describe how the smell of roses differs from, say, freesias.

Children can help to set up this activity by choosing a sensory mode and then bringing two or three similar things for comparison to the classroom.

- Descriptions of colour. Show the class a chart of colours and their names.

The most common way of tagging a colour is by matching it with an object that shares the colour or is a similar shade. Thus we have flamingo, charcoal, rose, pewter, ocean, butter, ivory and many more. Ask children to extend the list.

Add one or two adjectives to focus in on a particular shade. So we might have tomato red, dark olive, deep charcoal grey, chestnut brown, lagoon blue, amethyst purple and so on. Ask children to come up with further examples. Here also is an opportunity to discuss whether, with a colour like 'tomato red', the word 'tomato' (usually a noun) has now become an adjective describing that particular shade of red or whether the two words together name the colour (a noun phrase).

Ask children to pick a colour name they aren't familiar with and research it, finding one or more examples of things of that colour – for instance, alabaster, beige, chartreuse, dun, greige (we didn't know that one either!), magenta, taupe, teal, umber.

Highlight links between colour and emotions and moods. We are all familiar with feeling blue, being green with envy, white with shock or fear, seeing red and so on. Show children a list of colour words (with pictures of the colours if you wish) and ask what emotions or moods they might suggest. Similarly, show the class this list of emotions and ask which colours could be associated with them. There are no simple single right answers to these – annoyance, apathy, awe, bitterness, boredom, concern, confidence, courage, curiosity, delight, eagerness, fascination, frustration, happiness, hope, loneliness, love, optimism, pride, respect, sadness, smugness, sorrow, unease, wonderment.

Help children to deepen their understanding of these emotions by thinking of situations where they would be evoked. Some children might experience a spontaneous mental image of colour as they think about some of them. They might not be able to rationalise the connection but experience it rather as a hunch or intuition. For instance, we always link curiosity with buttercup yellow and awe with purple. We can't explain this but recognise that there are likely to be one or more subconscious reasons for the association.

Show the children a colour wheel. Ask the class to run their gaze slowly around it and to notice if moods or associations with moods come to mind. Allow time then to share impressions.

Tip: You can use the anchoring technique to reinforce a link between positive emotions and the colours they are associated with. So if a child links happiness with aquamarine, let's say, encourage her to think of that colour whenever she feels happy. Subsequently, encourage her to bring that colour to mind (or find an actual example) to evoke a feeling of happiness. Anchoring is a powerful technique for developing emotional resourcefulness.

- Synaesthesia. We return here to the idea of cross-matching sensory impressions (see also page 65). Colours are often described using physical references: ablaze, clashing, clean, cold, crisp, deep, earthy, electric, flaming, frosty, harsh, hot, icy, loud, muted, soft, solid, splashy, strong, violent, warm, watery.

Ask the class to brainstorm further connections. Try focussing on natural events and processes to kickstart the task – stormy grey, lightning white, sunset red, etc. As with the outcomes of most brainstorming sessions, some of the ideas won't work at all while others will be startlingly effective. Note that the trick of successful brainstorming is (a) not to *try* and think of ideas but just 'say it as you think it' and (b) not to analyse or judge thoughts as they appear – simply let them spill out of the mouth.

- Associations also play an important part in talking about colour. So for black we might have bat black, coal black, inky black, midnight black, sooty black, tar black, etc.

Ask children to think of other things that are black and see how well they work as descriptors. Extend the activity to other colours (try kathysteinemann.com for many more suggestions).

The next step is to consider the associations between colours and objects and select what is appropriate for the context of the writing. So, for instance, if we described a bride's bat black hair, the associations might come to mind of 'an old bat', 'batty', 'as blind as a bat' and so forth, which might not be what the writer intended. If the same character turned up at a Halloween party, however, the link would be apt.

Figure 39.1 Word cloud – colour association white

Sift through the children's brainstormed associations, pick some of them and decide which would be appropriate contexts or situations for describing colours in that way.

Introduce or revisit similes, which form another useful descriptive technique. Begin with the 'as' pattern – The woman's hair was as black as midnight.

Tip: You can combine this with other descriptive techniques explored next. Adding alliteration would give us, the woman's hair was as black as a moonless midnight.

Also try the 'like' pattern – The woman's hair was black, like a midnight sky. Go through various colour associations, framing them as similes.

- Colours also carry symbolic associations in some cultures and philosophical traditions. Red for instance has been associated with danger, courage, strength, energy, the power of life and passion (Ref: Ozaniec (1997)).

Researching colour symbolism can be a task that children undertake for themselves. Doing so will deepen their understanding of symbols, highlight metaphorical thinking, exercise the imagination and boost children's vocabulary.

- Collections of symbols/associations can be represented visually as word clouds (Figure 39.1). These are apps that you can use to group associated words into a variety of shapes, colours, frequency of use in selected text, etc. Displaying word clouds makes vocabulary 'visually available': children will glance at the display often, increasing their chances of absorbing the spellings of the featured words. A free online word cloud generator can be found at www.wordclouds.com/.

CHAPTER

Some literary devices for descriptive writing

Many techniques are available for making descriptions more vivid – key the section heading into a search engine for a comprehensive list. Some of the commoner ones are as follows.

Adjectives. The main points to bear in mind when using adjectives are to choose them carefully and use them sparingly. Adjectives used effectively enhance a piece of writing. If they are used too liberally they become tedious. As an adjunct to this, only two or at most three adjectives should be tagged to any given noun.

Adverbs. These are one of the four 'content' parts of speech (along with nouns, adjectives and verbs). They add to and clarify verbs and thus are not just useful but often necessary. As with adjectives however they must be used discerningly, following the principle of less is more. As a rule of thumb, encourage children to ask themselves if any adverb really does add information to a sentence; in other words, they should consider how much work a word or phrase does. For instance, 'The man spoke in a language that Anna couldn't understand. Obviously, she was confused'. Here, 'obviously' adds nothing to the sentence. Other adverbs that need to be similarly assessed include interestingly, clearly, actually and literally. The final example refers to something that is not figuratively or metaphorically the case but all too often is used as though it were so. To say 'it was literally raining cats and dogs' means that cats and dogs were *really* falling from the sky. But to say 'the large diamond was literally worth a million pounds' is correct, if that was in fact the value of the jewel.

Use proverbs to emphasise the point. Ask children to insert 'literally' into each of these sentences and decide in which of them the adverb is used correctly.

1. You can lead a horse to water but you cannot make it drink.
2. A man's home is his castle.
3. Christmas comes but once a year.
4. Every cloud has a silver lining.

5. Half a loaf is better than no bread.
6. Rome was not built in a day.

Note: Where a proverb can be literally true, discuss with the class what it might also mean figuratively.

Alliteration. These days alliteration refers to the repetition of consonant sounds (in Old English verse it also included vowel sounds, which today we term assonance). Alliteration therefore contributes to the aural quality of sentences. Where this is pleasing to the ear it comes under the umbrella term of euphony (from the Greek euphōnos, meaning 'well sounding'). Where it grates on the ear it is called cacophony (ill sounding). Encourage children to read out loud, including their own work, to draw out the aural qualities of the language.

Ask children to read these sentences aloud and decide which sound 'good' or pleasant and which are jarring or discordant. Note that it isn't necessary for children to understand what these examples mean as the emphasis is on the way they sound.

1. When Zeus stills the winds asleep in the solid drift (Homer's *The Iliad*).
2. From forth the fatal loins of these two foes/A pair of star-cross'd lovers take their life (Shakespeare's *Romeo and Juliet*, prologue).
3. With throats unslaked, with black lips baked,/Agape they heard me call (Coleridge's *Rime of the Ancient Mariner*).
4. Season of mists and mellow fruitfulness,/Close bosom-friend of the maturing sun;/Conspiring with him how to load and bless/With fruit the vines that round the thatch-eves run (Keats's 'To Autumn').
5. And being no stranger to the art of war, I have him a description of cannons, culverins, muskets, carabines, pistols, bullets, powder, swords, bayonets, battles, sieges, retreats, attacks, undermines, countermines, bombardments, sea-fights (Swift's *Gulliver's Travels*).

Connotations. These are ideas and feelings that are evoked in someone beyond the literal meanings of words. So for instance, while the words 'house' and 'home' literally refer to the same thing, house is a 'warmer' word that for most people evokes images of family, safety, security and comfort.

Ask children to discuss how they think these words differ in the ideas they bring to mind and the feelings they evoke. Note that connotations can be positive (e.g. vintage), negative (e.g. dilapidated) or neutral (e.g. old).

1. Childish, childlike, youthful
2. Curious, questioning, nosy
3. Thin, slender, skinny
4. Easygoing, relaxed, lazy

Figure 40.1 Connotations 1

5. Interested, obsessed, enquiring
6. Brash, confident, self-assured

The connotative influence of words and images is used extensively in advertising and the language of politics. (Note that a connotation is a suggested or implied meaning, deriving from the Latin 'to mark'. An association is a connection between two or more things. The word derives from the Latin 'to unite'.) Can the children

Some literary devices

Figure 40.2 Connotations 2

see any connotations in either category in the following examples (Figures 40.1 and 40.2)?

Pathetic fallacy. This is a form of personification, referring specifically to the attributing of human emotions to the landscape and the forces of nature. So we read of a raging storm, the ocean's fury, the merciless desert sun and so on. Use of this device heightens the atmosphere and mood of a description and can mirror or complement the emotional state of characters in a narrative.

- Ask the class to brainstorm a list of emotions/feelings/moods. Which ones lend themselves to pathetic fallacy?
- Create a mood gallery. Invite the children to bring in pictures of nature scenes. What feelings do they evoke? What words normally linked to human emotions could be used in a description of a chosen scene?

Repetition. In persuasive language and rhetoric, repetition serves to drive a point home. The 'power of three' is a common example of this, where an idea or phrase is repeated three times to highlight an issue or topic. The device is also found in nursery stories and fairy tales, such as 'The Three Little Pigs', 'The Three Billy Goats Gruff' and 'Goldilocks and the Three Bears'. In descriptive writing and poetry, repetition contributes to the aural quality of the language. So we might read about the clip-clop-clip-clop of a horse's hooves, the rat-a-tat-tat of a machine gun or the clang-clang-clang of a hammer on an anvil. As you see (or hear), repetition is often used with onomatopoeia.

- Ask children to list sounds associated with the picture in Figure 40.3.

Symbolism. This is where words and images represent or evoke a complex set of ideas. Another way of defining a symbol is that it's something that *goes beyond* the thing itself and in that sense it is different to a sign. So a rose for example can symbolise love and the vast range of associations that go with it, whereas a road sign indicating a 30-mile-an-hour speed limit is just that and nothing more.

- Look at a selection of national flags and discuss and/or research what the designs with their associated colours and images might represent (also see colour associations on page 115).
- Look at the logos of different companies and enterprises. What do they represent or say about the company or enterprise?

The word 'logo' comes from the Latin *loco*, meaning 'in place of, instead of, for' (Ref: Wiktionary.org accessed May 2020). Logos are usually quite simple visually so that they can be recognised immediately and become more effective over time.

Figure 40.3 Funfair

Some literary devices

Figure 40.4 Abstract shapes

- Ask children to discuss and decide what each of the images in Figure 40.4 could symbolise. There is not necessarily a single right answer.

Take it further:
Ask whether changing the orientation or otherwise altering a shape alters its symbolism. For example, could the double-arrowed line mean something different if it were first positioned horizontally and then vertically?

Some literary devices

Figure 40.5 Symbols

Encourage children to combine and/or colour the shapes to suggest further symbols, bearing in mind that colours can often be rich in associations.

Use objects from the natural world to generate ideas for symbols. Many aspects of nature already have many symbolic associations. Ask children to research some of these.

Check thoughtco.com for more.

- Spend some time talking to the children about abstract nouns related to concepts in preparation for the next activity. Abstract nouns name intangible things that are not directly perceived by the senses. So although we can perceive the process and consequences of justice, for example, the *idea* of justice exists only as a concept.

Note: Some of the big concepts that form the basis of philosophical enquiries are abstract nouns: fairness and equality, reality, justice, meaning and purpose, freedom, good and evil, beauty, truth – and the Big One, life and death.

See, for instance, Bowkett (2018); Buckley (2011); Laws (2002), (2006).

Some literary devices

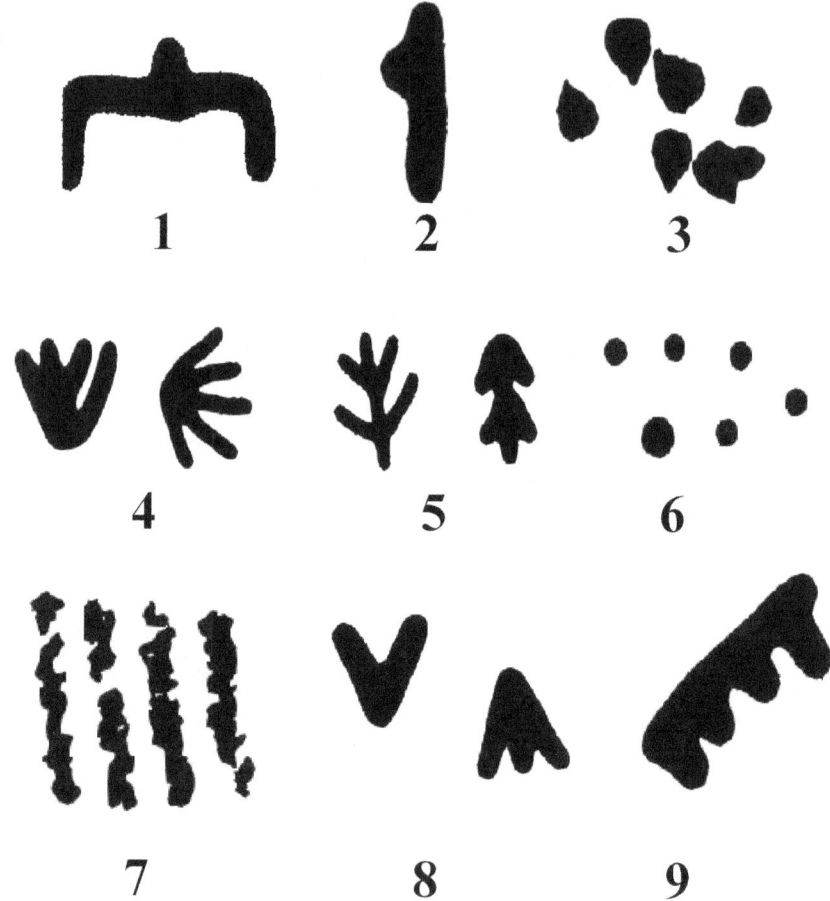

Figure 40.6 Rock art symbols

Source: Genevieve von Petzinger from her book 'The First Signs'

- Ask children to discuss/research what human rights-related symbols (Figure 40.5) mean. Their ideas can be displayed as an association web around each image.

  See conversations.marketing-partners.com for more.

- The images in Figure 40.6 are based on some of the earliest known examples of cave and rock art, dating back several tens of thousands of years. Their meanings are either not entirely clear or completely unknown. What suggestions can the children come up with? (Ref: von Petzinger (2016)).

CHAPTER

Pictograms and hieroglyphs

A pictogram is a simple image that directly represents the thing it is referring to. So the pictograph of a bee would actually be a simple drawing of a bee. Pictograms are also called pictographs and, more recently, icons. The advantage of pictographs is that they are recognisable irrespective of whichever language you speak. Even though the words for bee will vary from language to language, people from all countries will know at a glance what the bee pictograph refers to.

Expressing ideas pictorially is more difficult when those concepts are more abstract. One solution is to combine pictograms whose names sound out the concept you want to convey. So the idea of 'belief' for instance can be communicated by linking the pictograms of a bee and a leaf – bee-leaf. The disadvantage of this is that while that pictogram would work in English, it wouldn't in other languages. This is also the reason why researchers had difficulty translating Egyptian and Mayan languages since very little is known about the sounds represented by the images.

Most children will have seen Egyptian hieroglyphs. The term was first used by the ancient Greeks and means 'sacred carvings'. The earliest evidence of hieroglyphs dates back to 3300–3200 BC (Ref: history-world.org) and were used by the Egyptians for the next 3500 years.

Some hieroglyphs evolved into letters of our own alphabet. For instance, the letter K (Figure 41.1) underwent this transformation over many centuries.

Figure 41.1 Evolution of K

1 – The Egyptian hieroglyph for a hand dates back to 2000 BC.
2 – This is an early form of the letter itself, which was quicker and easier to draw than the hand shape. It comes from the Sinai alphabet and dates to 1750 BC.
3 – The Semitic form of the letter disregarded the meaning of the earlier hieroglyph, using the word for hand – kaph – as the basis for the further transformation into the letter we know today.
4 – The fourth image is from the Phoenician alphabet of around 800 BC.
5 – The modern K.
(Ref: Sacks (2003))

K is typical of the evolution of many letters, where more complex images changed into simpler yet more abstract forms. The Egyptian hieroglyph has a direct correspondence with an actual hand, whereas the modern K has no connection and instead is an image representing a sound.

Just as we put letters together to form words and then phrases and sentences[1], the Egyptians combined hieroglyphs to create more elaborate meanings. For instance, see Figure 41.2.

The first glyph represents movement, the second means to give directions and the third means approach. The significance of the legs is clear enough: you might ask the children how the other shapes contribute to the meaning of the glyph-combinations.

- Ask children, individually or in small groups, to design simple glyphs/pictures to represent the following: cat, aeroplane, flower, smartphone, forest, birthday, school, night, illness, dream – and other ideas of their own.

Take it further:

- Instruct each child or group to choose one of the nouns presented earlier and think of an adjective to go with it – big cat, jet aeroplane, colourful flower, etc. –

Figure 41.2 Hieroglyphs

and then to write the adjective on a scrap of paper. Now children are to swap scraps and design a glyph to represent the adjective-plus-noun combination.

Hieroglyphic conversion apps are available online, such as discoveringegypt.com. Some require a subscription, though the Penn Museum site lets you create your name in hieroglyphics for free (Figure 41.3). Have fun.

- Design glyphs to represent the following sentences. Advise children to keep the images as clear and simple as possible.

  A bird flew over the mountain.
  The street was crowded with people.
  Happy birthday.
  A year passes so quickly.
  Knowledge is power.

Take it further by asking children to come up with sentences of their own. As a class, discuss which glyph combinations might work best and why.

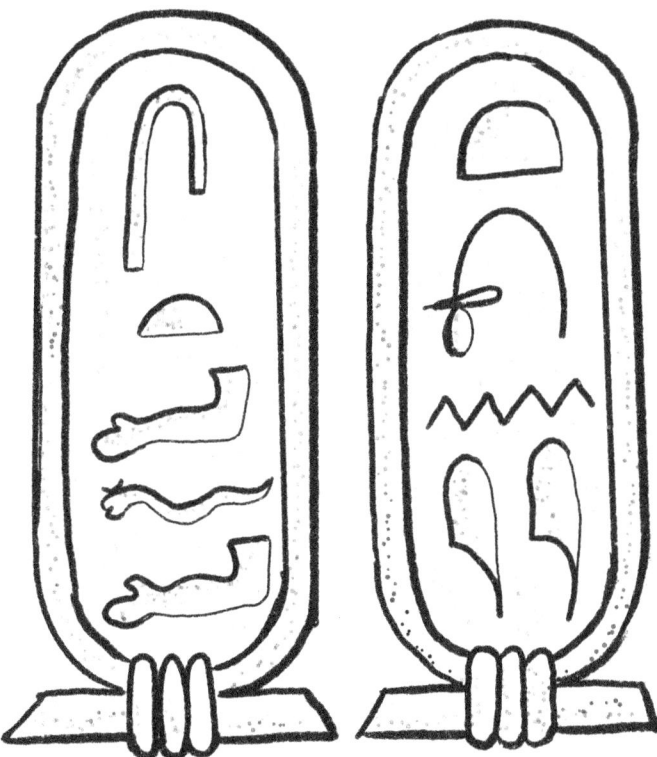

Figure 41.3 Cartouches of Steve and Tony

Pictograms and hieroglyphs

- Take a simple sentence like the following: 'The cat sat on the mat'. Working collaboratively or alone, instruct the children to design a suitable glyph to represent this idea.

    Now, ask for adjectives to describe the cat. Collect about ten of these.
    Ask for adverbs to tell us more about 'sat'.
    Collect more prepositions, so, as well as on, under, above, beside, around, etc.

Split the class into groups and instruct each group to create a new and more elaborate sentence by choosing from the selection of adjectives, adverbs and prepositions. Design a glyph to represent the new sentence.

- Give the class a selection of the infinitive form of some verbs either from this list or others that yourself and the children have supplied: to cry, to dance, to celebrate, to think, to believe, to understand. Design glyphs to represent these.
- Taking symbolism a little further, the statue in the illustration in Figure 41.4 plays into how we might 'read' the picture. We have no idea whether the woman is watching someone leave, waiting for someone to come or witnessing an event below. The statue, however, has a symbolic weight independent of the picture.

Figure 41.4 Love and Justice

Pictograms and hieroglyphs

Figure 41.5 Demon, cupid, warrior and praying figure

The statue is Lady Justice, representing the more abstract notion of justice and the law. Ask children to suggest why she is blindfolded and carries a sword and scales. (Interestingly, the statue of Lady Justice atop the Old Bailey courthouse in London stands without a blindfold. According to Wikipedia (accessed July 2020), the courthouse brochure explains that this is because originally Lady Justice was not blindfolded, while her maidenly form suggests that she is impartial, making a blindfold unnecessary. There is an opportunity here to discuss whether or how someone's appearance can influence other's opinions. Indeed, the topic of sexism and stereotypes can also be discussed, the aggressive warrior is male, the passive figure at prayer female.)

Ask the children to discuss that if there was a different statue, such as one of the ones in Figure 41.5 (a demon, a cupid, a warrior or a praying figure), how might that affect how we perceive the picture?

- Now move on to more abstract ideas such as charity, freedom, love, generosity, uncertainty, creativity, compassion, envy. Can children design glyphs that represent these?

Note

1. Our alphabet is amazingly economical. There are but 26 letters and 44 phonemes (some sources say 42) that can be combined to create the quarter-million or so words in our language (both current and obsolete, according to oxforddictionaries.com, though sources vary over the estimated number), which in turn can be put together to generate *countless* sentences. This is known as infinite generativity, a feature likely shared by all human languages. Incidentally, the word 'alphabet' itself comes from the names of the first two letters of the Greek alphabet, alpha and beta.

CHAPTER

Letter associations

The capital A is associated with beginnings, being the first letter of the alphabet, with superiority as in first class and with success as in getting an A grade in school.

- As a class activity, pick other letters one at a time and ask the children to brainstorm as many associations as they can think of in a given time.

Tip: David Sacks's book *The Alphabet* is a useful source of ideas if children are struggling.

- Some phonemes are associated with clusters of words and suggest a meaning that some linguists think is inherent in the phoneme itself (though this is a controversial theory that is not widely accepted). The term 'phonaestheme' refers to the pairing of meaning and form in a language.

So, for instance, /b/ is associated with round things, including ball, balloon, bangle, bead, belly, bladder, blob, bowl.

Ask children if they can add associated words to the following lists:

/cr/ suggesting pressure or breaking: crush, crumble, crack, etc.
/fl/ suggesting movement: flap, flee, flick, flow, flutter, etc.
/gl/ suggesting mainly reflected or indirect light: glare, gleam, glimmer, etc.
/gl/ suggesting reflecting surfaces: glacier, glass, etc.
/sn/ being associated with the nose: sniffle, snore, snuffle, snout, etc.

See Magnus (2010); Mitchell (2006) and thoughtco.com for more ideas.

CHAPTER

Describing phonemes

Language is only possible because of the versatility of the human vocal apparatus. Formal teaching of phonics plus checks and assessments of children's phonemic awareness still forms part of the UK National Curriculum, though a more informal approach can also contribute to children's understanding of how sounds link to letters, syllables and words. The idea of 'playing' with sounds is similar to the notion of developing children's creative writing and narrative understanding through exploration and experiment rather than by systematically learning and rigidly applying a raft of 'writing rules' (though we recognise the importance of teaching children formally about spelling, punctuation and grammar).

- Ask children to name the parts of themselves that allow us to make sounds and create words: lungs, throat, tongue, teeth, roof of the mouth, etc. Note that some children might include aspects of facial expression and body language. Show the class a cutaway diagram of the human organs of speech to introduce children to the more technical names, such as diaphragm, trachea, larynx, soft palate, nasal cavity.
- Ask for volunteers to speak a chosen phoneme and ask classmates to listen carefully to check for different pronunciations – the dyslexia-reading-well.com website has a useful chart of phonemes and a guide to their pronunciation, and there are also YouTube videos that will allow children to hear how the different phonemes sound.

Note: There is an opportunity here to discuss accent and dialect with your class.

- Split the class into pairs or small groups. Give each group a word to 'play with'; to speak aloud and notice how the vocal apparatus produces it. Encourage children to write a short description of this. Subsequently, ask each group to share their word and description with their classmates.

Describing phonemes

Take this further by enriching the children's vocabulary when describing the sounds of words and parts of words. So for instance, to us the verb 'duck' is sort of 'heavy'. The /d/ has a 'downward' kind of feel to it, which we notice in words like mud, dump, dunk. The /u/ reinforces this and reminds us of 'under' (but not 'up'!). The consonant blend /fl/ in the word 'flat' makes us think of slipperiness and sliding, while the /a/ makes an abrupt flat kind of sound. Also, saying the whole word makes us want to sweep our hand as though across a flat surface. The /t/ suggests a sudden stop to this movement.

Note that these are subjective impressions. Children will have different ideas. The point of the activity is to raise awareness of how sounds link to syllables and how these are produced by the vocal apparatus and by face and body movement. Also see McGuinness (1998).

CHAPTER

Interpreting abstract shapes

We've already looked at this in the sections on symbols, early rock art, pictograms and hieroglyphs, but we now want to focus on using abstract shapes to think about characters that children can use in their stories and to think about emotions, personality traits and values.

The technique involves two leaps of the imagination. Show the class one of the shapes and ask the following:

What could this be and what does it remind you of?

If this told us something about our character what would we learn?

- So, using the following image (Figure 44.1), we could ask the two questions, with the second being, 'If this told us something about our character's dark side or bad qualities, what would we learn?'

A child might respond, 'It reminds me of a crescent moon, but it's also broken. When the moon is a crescent, most of what we see of it is dark, so I think the character's dark side is a large part of him. And I think he might have weaknesses – parts of his personality that are broken or damaged'.

Using the image in Figure 44.2, we could say it tells us something about the character's future.

One response might be that our character feels walled in but on thinking about it realises that there are a number of ways out of his current situation.

If Figure 44.3 told us something about our character's relationships, we could say that for various reasons (that we can use other abstract images to explore), our character's relationships always seem to 'spiral downwards' until they reach a dead end. Or looking at it the other way, relationships could be ever-expanding, as our character and his friends learn more and more about each other.

- Use the selection of images in Figure 44.4 and ask the children to go through the two-step process to learn more about a character they're inventing from scratch or one they're currently writing about.

DOI: 10.4324/9781003184003-44

Interpreting abstract shapes

Figure 44.1 Character traits 1

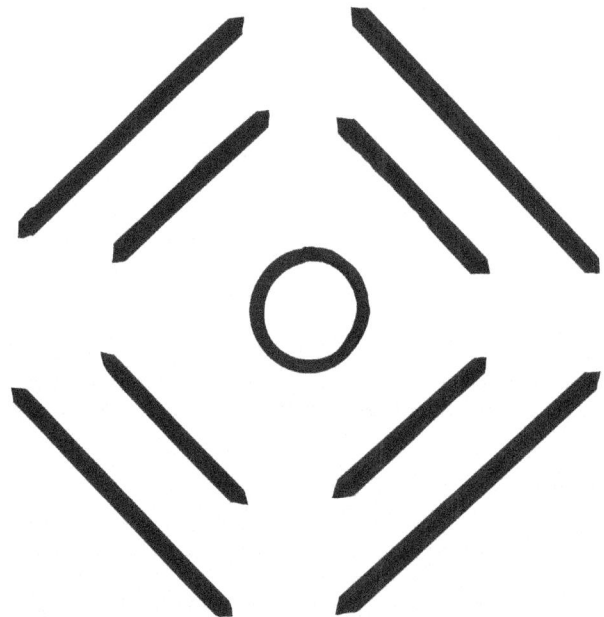

Figure 44.2 Character traits 2

Interpreting abstract shapes

Figure 44.3 Character traits 3

- You can work the activity the other way round. What simple abstract images can children think of to represent these emotions and traits visually? Note that images must be abstract, so anger can't be represented by a fist or people fighting, though the image in Figure 44.5 would be acceptable (ask the children why).

Traits

1. Careful
2. Patient
3. Confident
4. Mean
5. Determined

Interpreting abstract shapes

Figure 44.4 Abstract emotions

Figure 44.5 Abstract anger

6. Independent
7. Bossy
8. Brave
9. Thoughtful
10. Proud

Feelings

a) Shocked
b) Annoyed
c) Jealous
d) Embarrassed
e) Angry
f) Scared
g) Worried
h) Uneasy
i) Sad
j) Disappointed

- Abstract images can also be used to explore human values and rights. How would children, using simple designs, represent independence, challenge, achievement, power, tradition, respect, freedom of thought, freedom of expression, marriage and family, democracy, play, food and shelter, education, fairness, responsibility (these being some of the basic human rights)?

CHAPTER

Venn diagrams

A Venn diagram shows, usually by overlapping circles, the relationships between groups of objects or ideas that have something in common. It was devised by mathematician and philosopher John Venn around 1880. For our purposes we'll tweak the idea and use it in the context of character development and genre-blending in fiction.

- Characters. Draw a large circle to represent the mind/personality of a character. Cut out smaller circles to represent traits, feelings and issues going on in that person's life. The size of the subsidiary circles indicates the importance of the issue or feeling. If two subsidiary circles overlap, then they are influencing one another in some discernible way – i.e. in a way recognised by that person. Subsidiary circles that overlap the boundary of the main circle represent issues and feelings that are being openly expressed by the individual. Subsidiary circles placed near the centre of the main circle exist at a subconscious level – that is to say, they will still influence that person's behaviour but will not be recognised, or only partially realised, by the individual.

Using some of the feelings and traits listed on pages 135 and 137, a visual representation of a character at a particular point in time is presented in Figure 45.1.

Character profiles can be built up over time or created in a single session by individual children or groups. The benefits of planning in this way are that children need to think about the 'inner world' of their characters rather than focussing only on outward appearance, and they need to consider traits and feelings as dynamic forces operating within a character's psyche. Subsidiary circles can be made from different colours of paper, linking emotions with colour. Children can also draw on them rather than just writing the name of the feeling or trait.

Take it further:

Ideally, the main characters in a story will change over time. The idea of a 'journey' within a story can refer to a physical journey, but it also means a transformative

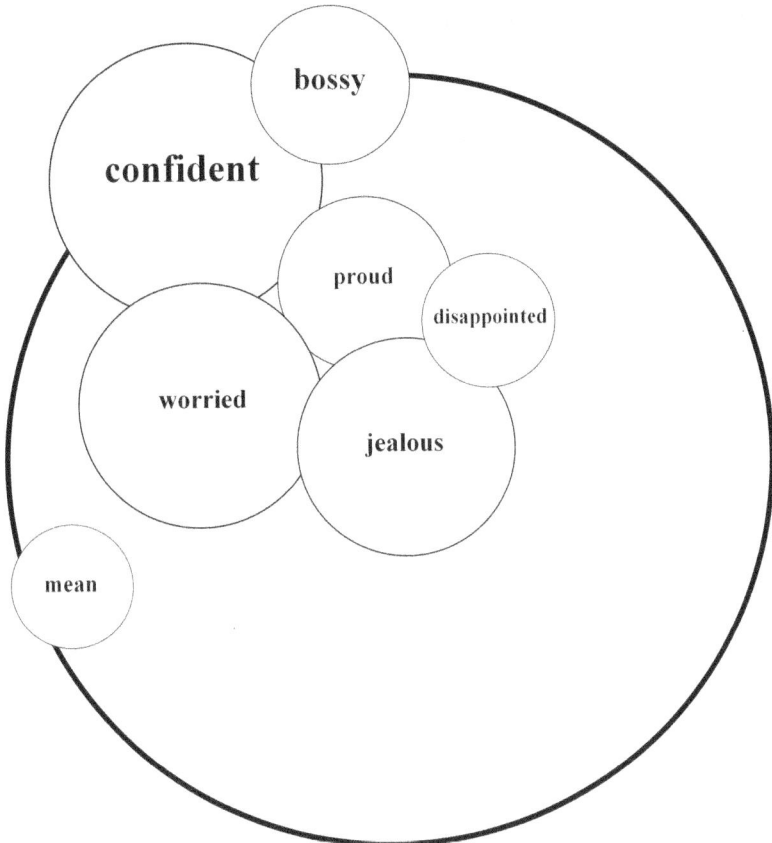

Figure 45.1 Overlapping circles

experience. Ask children to create two diagrams of the same character, one representing that person at the beginning of their chosen story and the other showing how the character has changed by the end. The stories can be ones written by the children themselves, novels they've read or those you've studied with the class.

A variation of the aforementioned idea is to present children with the before and after diagrams and then build a story around them. To do this, children will need to think about the genre they want to write in and the outward appearance of their character before plotting in more detail.

Once children have created a character profile, show them a number of situations and events. How would their characters react in those circumstances, and how might any circumstance alter a character's psychological profile?

Ask children to work in pairs. If their two characters met, how would they react to one another at the outset – i.e. what would their first impressions be? Now put them in a particular situation. How would they react to/influence one another?

The circle technique can also be used in the context of emotional resourcefulness. Children can create profiles of themselves (which they may want to keep completely private), exploring their own feelings as they do so. As a thought experiment, suggest that moving the subsidiary circles around changes the dynamic of any given feeling and can alter the relationship that one feeling might have on others. Also, changing the size and colour of subsidiary circles, as well as their position, changes how a feeling is experienced. So if a large red circle representing anger was replaced by a smaller and less brightly coloured one, this can have a real effect on the actual anger a child may be experiencing. Manipulating the circles in this way is a visual metaphor for changes that a child desires: consciously using the technique can trigger subconscious processes to effect change.

- Overlapping genres. All fictional genres have their own motifs and conventions. A motif, or trope, is a constituent feature that helps to define the genre in which it is used. Motifs can therefore be people, places, objects, scenarios and sequences of dialogue. When they appear in ways that readers expect, we can say that they are being used conventionally, true to the conventions of the genre. So a brave knight slaying the dragon, or a flying saucer landing on the White House lawn, are motifs being used conventionally within the genres of Fantasy and Science Fiction respectively. Check children's understanding of these ideas by asking, 'How do we recognise a fantasy story?'

Standard advice for writers is to learn the conventions of a chosen genre before attempting to use motifs *un*conventionally. Cut out a large circle of paper and decide which genre it will represent. Ask children to create a visual display by drawing and labelling motifs that appear in that genre and then placing them within the circle.

Mixing motifs found in different genres can generate fresh ideas for stories. Represent this visually by overlapping two circles, say Fantasy and Science Fiction. Select some motifs from each genre and move them into the overlap area. What story ideas now suggest themselves? The 'heads or tails' technique on page 143 can help with this.

For more ideas about overlapping genres, see Bowkett and Hitchman (2012).

CHAPTER

'Sliderman'

Another way of thinking about characters (or oneself) is to use a template like the one in Figure 46.1.

Invite children to add their own selection of traits and emotions. Also, they can consider where along the number line to mark each emotion or use dice rolls to choose randomly. Characters created in this way sometimes throw up unexpected and original combinations of traits, sparking further thoughts about relationships and events in the story.

Tip: Suggest using counters or thin strips of paper that can be freely moved along the 'trait lines' rather than making pencil or pen marks. In this way, children can change their characters' profiles in light of further thought, emphasizing the idea that characters change throughout a story.

> How would a sliderman character behave in a given situation?
> How would two such characters react to one another?
> Pick a topic for a conversation. Put children into pairs. What would their characters say to one another?
> Put a character into a genre. Does he/she now need to change because of that?
> Deliberately highlight or create contradictions in a character profile and ask the children to come up with reasonable explanations. So, for instance, how could a character be very shy yet have many friends? How could a character be both sensitive and bossy? How can we account for a character being kind but pessimistic?

Name:	Physical description:
Image:	

Strengths:	Weaknesses:

                                 1   2   3   4   5   6

Intelligence - _____

                   _____

                   _____

                   _____

                   _____

                   _____

                   _____

Figure 46.1 Sliderman

Copyright material from Steve Bowkett and Tony Hitchman (2022), *Visualising Literacy and How to Teach It*, Routledge

CHAPTER

Heads or tails

This activity is deceptively simple and works on the notion that introducing a random element to the creative process generates fresh ideas, or as we like to say, the game helps to 'take your mind by surprise'.

Using a picture as a stimulus, children ask a series of closed questions and toss a two-colour counter or a coin to obtain a yes or no answer. While the child is responsible for the question (more on this next), she or he does not need to have any fear of getting the answer wrong, which makes the game feel safe. A 'yes' response adds a piece of information to the material that the child can use later. A 'no' answer means that the child must think of another question.

When introducing the technique, offer the following instructions:

a) Questions must be relevant and appropriate – i.e. no frivolous or silly questions.
b) The technique must not be used to ask questions about classmates or any other actual person. (Some children are tempted to subvert the game by asking personal and sometimes inappropriate questions.)
c) Everyone must flip the counter sensibly. Simply dropping it from shoulder height onto a tabletop is sufficient (you don't want counters flying all over the room).
d) Demonstrate the game to the whole class initially. As such, questions must be fairly general – i.e. not relating to any genre. Although you might offer children a selection of pictures to choose from when they are working individually or in groups after the demo, some children will want to use the picture you first show them. As such, questions should not 'force' them in a certain direction. For example, using the cat picture on page 12, asking, 'Is the light in the sky a dragon's fiery breath?' should be discouraged because if the answer is yes, all children are then 'locked' into planning a fantasy story. An alternative ploy is to allow genre-specific questions, but if children subsequently want to use that same picture, instruct them to edit out any information that prevents them from taking their own direction.

e) Questions must be framed such that yes answers add to the story-in-the-making and support its logical consistency. If a child asked, 'Is the cat purple?' (see page 32), *before tossing the counter*, the child must come up with a reasonable scenario such that if the cat is purple, then it's for a good reason that contributes usefully to the narrative.

f) Once a yes or no answer is given, it must be accepted. Children cannot 'try again' to obtain a different answer. However, if a child comes up with a strong idea – one that is relevant and develops the narrative – you can advise her simply to decide on the answer she wants and not to 'gamble' by flipping the counter.

g) Contradictory questions are unacceptable. So if a child gets a yes to the question, 'Is it night-time?' no one can then ask if it's daytime.

h) Instruct children that they don't need to write out the questions. If the answer to a question is no, in most cases they won't need to write anything. So using our cat picture, if we asked, 'Is the cat frightened?' and the answer is no, there would be no point in recording that piece of non-information. However, children should record yes answers in note form. So, 'Is the cat angry?' If the answer is yes a child need only jot down 'cat is angry'. This is another example of the minimal writing strategy we looked at elsewhere (page 57). Reluctant writers may be more inclined to join in if they realise they don't actually have to write much at this stage.

Those are the basic rules. As you'll appreciate, the activity is applicable across a wide age and ability range (and is an example of the principle of differentiation by outcome rather than differentiation of materials). Also, children can work alone or in groups. If working in groups, instruct children that once a question has been asked, that child must pass the counter on to the next person. This prevents anyone from dominating the activity. It's fine if a child doesn't have a question in mind, but when her turn comes the counter must be passed to her to signify that she is still a valued member of the group. She can then pass on the counter to the next person.

Some children will only need to play the game for a short while to gather enough ideas to start a story. They then usually ask if they can go and write now, and we recommend this. Other children like to stay with the activity longer.

Here are some further tips:

1. Some teachers feel that closed questioning has limited value. But like any other form of questioning, it's a tool that can be useful in particular contexts, such as in our counter-flip game. If you say to a child, 'Do you like reading?' then either a yes or a no reply gives relatively little information. Closed questioning is also associated with convergent thinking, which is somehow seen as 'inferior' to divergent thinking that opens out enquiry and, naturally, is linked with more open questions – 'What is it about reading that you like?'

2. However, open questions might also leave a child floundering if she doesn't have strategies to help her to think. Asking 'What story could this picture be telling?' can be just as limiting as a closed question if the child doesn't know *how* to think it through (we're back to the 'go away and think about it' issue).
3. The counter-flip game exploits the best of both worlds because of the following:

Closed questions focus the attention on particular details or aspects of the topic, allowing for the exploration of small details within the narrative.

Open questions can be 'translated' into a series of closed questions (more on this next).

Closed questions break a large complex task (What could this story be about?) into smaller and more manageable steps.

Closed questions generate information that is assimilated bit by bit as the questioning proceeds. Open questions often call for the immediate assimilation of lots of information, which can leave a child tongue-tied or overwhelmed.

The information generated by closed questioning, once assimilated, can be used for responding subsequently to open questions.

4. The counter-flip technique leads to an endpoint in speculative enquiry. Thinking back to the maybe hand (page 16), the children thought of at least five possible explanations for the cat being frightened. Flipping the counter allows us to settle on one of them for the purpose of working out what might be happening in the story. Alternatively, a child can pick an option without using the counter if it fits with her or his story-in-the-making.
5. Flipping the counter brings a double benefit. If a child asks, 'Is it a big dog frightening the cat?' and the answer is yes, then the earlier speculation has resulted in a conclusion, an idea that the child can utilise at once. If the answer is no, then progress has already been made because one possibility has been discounted[1]. And it's perfectly safe for the child to flip the coin to find out what else might be frightening the cat – insofar as she can't get a 'wrong' answer.

When the counter comes up no, tell the whole class or the child that asked the question that that idea isn't lost: 'We can put it in the treasure box of ideas to use another time'. This makes clear the principle that no idea is wasted. The 'no' simply means that a particular idea won't be used right now. To emphasise this, have a box (labelled 'Treasure Box of Ideas') on hand. When the counter indicates no, suggest to the child who asked the question – or a volunteer scribe – to make a quick note of it on a scrap of paper and drop it into the box for later use. Allow children free access to the ideas box whenever they need it. You can also run more formal sessions by selecting an idea yourself to use as the basis for discussion prior to getting the class to do some creative writing.

6. The game utilises the element of randomness and chance. This leads the questioner away from routine thinking skills ('and then' thinking, see page 18) and allows her to have unanticipated thoughts. When the child herself doesn't quite know where the questions will lead, she is likely to remain interested and engaged for longer (the 'what happens next?' principle).
7. Subsequent questions are informed by previous answers. So if a big dog is frightening the cat, does that mean the dog's running free? If the counter comes up yes that leads naturally to wonder how come the dog is on the loose. If the answer is no that prompts the questioner to wonder why the dog's owner is allowing his animal to terrify the cat. The child quickly builds up a platform of information by assimilating an increasing number of interconnected and logically consistent ideas as time goes by.

A few further tips:

Avoid feeding the children questions – let them do the thinking. But you can guide and prompt by saying things like I wonder what kind (genre) of story you'd like this to be? I wonder who lives in that house and what they might look like. What else might be happening in the town?

Help children to translate open questions into closed questions. Big question words are where, when, what, why, who and how (also 'which' if that helps). Give children practice with these before the counter-flipping begins. Choosing a picture, ask the class how many who-questions they can think of, how many what-questions, etc. These can then be broken down into closed questions. So 'Who lives in the house?' can be turned into, 'Does a family live in the house?' 'Are there any children living in the house?' and so on.

It's useful to have a follow-on activity ready as groups will finish coin flipping at different times. Another option is to put a time limit on the activity; 10–15 minutes works well, although some children want to carry on beyond that. Or you can specify a focus for the counter-flipping: find out five things about someone living in the house; discover seven interesting things about what happened in the town earlier that day, etc.

It's not often that a child will get 'stuck' playing this game, but if one does offer guidelines rather than giving the child actual questions. So you might say, 'Would it be useful to find out something about one of the main characters?' Or, 'I'd like more information about the setting for this story'. Gentle prompting like this usually gives the child a sense of direction for asking fresh questions while retaining ownership of the activity.

Don't let children become a slave to tossing the counter. Sometimes you'll hear a child ask a question, flip the counter and then say, 'Oh, but I wanted that to be a yes!' This indicates that the child knows her own mind. After giving children their first experience of the game, encourage them to use the counter more discerningly. One way of doing this is to listen in on a group and at an opportune moment intervene by saying, 'Now that's a really good question. You can gamble it by flipping the counter or *decide for yourself* what you want the answer to be. If you do that, I'd be interested to know the reason for your choice'. Some children will still want to risk losing their preferred answer, which gives you the opportunity to point out the dangers of gambling!

As an extension of the previous point, encourage children to use the if-then pattern of thinking to consider the possible consequences of their questions before flipping the counter. So if a child wants to ask, 'Does the hero get injured?' prompt further thought by asking how that could affect other characters or how the injury might alter the hero's role in the story.

With questions like, 'Does the hero get injured?' you can increase the sophistication of the random approach by introducing dice rolls to find out *how badly* the hero is injured should the counter produce a yes answer. So 1 would indicate minimal injury and 6 would mean serious injury. Again, ask children to consider the possible consequences before rolling the die.

Encourage children to generate further closed questions by starting with open ones. By asking, 'When does the story take place?' you are prompting children to ask about when in history the story happens (narrowing this down beforehand if there are any relevant clues in the picture), at what time of year the story opens, what time of the day or night, etc.

The counter-flip game can also be used with the storyline planning technique (page 100). Place one of the words or pictures anywhere along the narrative line and then run the game. This makes the point that a picture or prompt-word doesn't have to represent the start of a story. In fact, placing the word or picture somewhere other than at the beginning means that children have to 'work backwards' to flesh out earlier sections of the narrative, as well as explore subsequent events.

Heads or tails is also a useful way to help children if their ideas dry up *during* the writing itself. Sometimes a child will launch into a story with a surge of enthusiasm, only to come to a dead end later. Should this happen, invite the child to pause and run the counter-flip game for a short while, basing questions on what has already been written. This is often sufficient to kickstart the child's imagination and get the writing going again.

Other useful questions children can ask once they have some information are as follows: 'What might happen next?' And 'How might the story end?' That first question can be used in conjunction with the maybe hand (page 16), where children think of at least five possible scenarios before choosing one they like, either by deciding for themselves or using a dice roll. The second question is useful if children have used counter-flips to work out how the story begins but have not yet explored further. Having a solid story beginning and a possible ending often makes filling in the middle much easier, acting as they do as reference points for further questions.

Take it further:

- Summarising. After groups have had a chance to learn more about the picture and how it relates to their story, ask children to summarise what they know in a given number of paragraphs or sentences. You can focus the task even more finely by giving instructions such as the following:

Tell me three interesting things about a person who lives nearby.

(If they have an idea of street layout) Write some directions to get me from this corner to the nearest medical centre (see also the visualisation work on page 72).

Explore a garden close by – talk it through with your friends and flip the counter if you need to – then draw a plan of the garden.

When children have accumulated some information, ask them to decide which facts are the most useful in helping them with their stories. This introduces criteria of relevance into the game and develops children's ability to ask quality questions.

Tell the children that this time they can flip the counter to answer their first question, but then *they* decide on the answer to the second question (based on a reason they've considered). This pattern of flip-then-choose-for-yourself begins to shift decision making onto the children and helps to train them to become more independent in their judgements.

The way the question is framed can influence the answer. One boy, Karl, loved to put zombies in every story he wrote. He asked, 'Is there a zombie behind the wall?' The coin came up no. He pondered this for a moment then asked, 'Will there be a zombie behind the wall in five minutes?' Even though the counter gave him a second no, he'd worked out how he could reframe his question to obtain the outcome he wanted. You can make this idea explicit for the children, extending their understanding by looking at how questionnaires and surveys are put together, where the way questions are framed nudge participants towards particular responses.

Use the game to find out more about other stories the children have read. Take a short story or an extract from a longer piece and flip to gather further information, in effect generating new plot ideas based on ones the children already know about.

If a description lacks detail, then suggest counter-flipping to create more. This helps children to develop their metacognition to the point where they can enrich their own imagined characters and settings as they read other people's work.

The same activity can be used with the children's own writing. Use a story that a child has willingly offered for this, since it requires a degree of self-confidence not to feel criticised or that their work is being 'picked on'. So for instance, if a young writer has written that his character was wearing a long coat, someone else in the class can ask, 'Was it a black coat?' and flip the counter. If the answer is no, the writer can either suggest a colour that would be in keeping with the character or, indeed argue the case – the child might want his character to wear black because he's the villain or because he's going to a funeral. If the answer is yes encourage the writer and classmates to come up with a few reasons why the decision fits with the story.

We must presume that every aspect of a professionally written story or poem is intentional. So if for instance a writer kills off a major character in Chapter 1, it will be for a good reason. Help the class to investigate the 'thinking behind the writing'. Why did the author get rid of an important character so early? Once the idea of author intention has been explored, play the counter-flip game to create alternative 'paths' through the narrative. What if Romeo and Juliet had not died at the end? What if Bilbo had not destroyed the ring? What if Darth Vader was not Luke's father?

After running the heads and tails activity a few times, do a question analysis with the class. Which questions proved most useful and why? Broadly speaking, useful questions include those which focus on and develop plot, characters and setting. But different groups will also come up with more specific questions that allow them to make good progress in their own particular narratives.

Note

1. It's unlikely that the counter will produce a run of five no's. But if it does, it's an opportunity to ask, 'So what else can we think of that might be frightening the cat?'

CHAPTER

Dice journey

To run this activity groups will need a large sheet of paper (light-coloured sugar paper works well), marker pens, a two-colour counter, a six-sided die and an eight-sided die. The eight-sided die is to determine direction using compass points (Figure 48.1).

The aim of the activity is to create a setting to be used in a story. Groups can begin literally from nothing, having no idea what their landscape will look like, or they may have discussed the plot and locations beforehand. Children can also determine the degree of randomness they build into their map-making, relying completely on dice rolls and counter-flips, or combining these with reasoning and inference as they create the landscape.

Let's suppose that a group of four children want to create a setting for a fantasy story. They have not talked about it beforehand and intend to build the landscape as they go along. They begin in the centre of their sheet of paper.

Pupil 1: So we want the story to have wizards and different creatures.

Pupil 2: How about dragons? (Nods from classmates)

Pupil 3: Dragons live in caves don't they and guard treasure?

Pupil 4: So we need some mountains if we're having caves. Shall I roll the die to see where the mountains are? (rolls eight-sided die) Two – northeast. I'll draw them in.

Pupil 2: How far away are they?

Pupil 1: A day's trek.

Pupil 3: That depends on the terrain. Let's find out in kilometres.

Pupil 4: Would they have kilometres in this world?

Pupil 3: It's just to give us an idea. I suggest we roll both dice and add the numbers, and that's how far away the mountains are. (rolls dice) Seven and five, so twelve kilometres away.

Dice journey

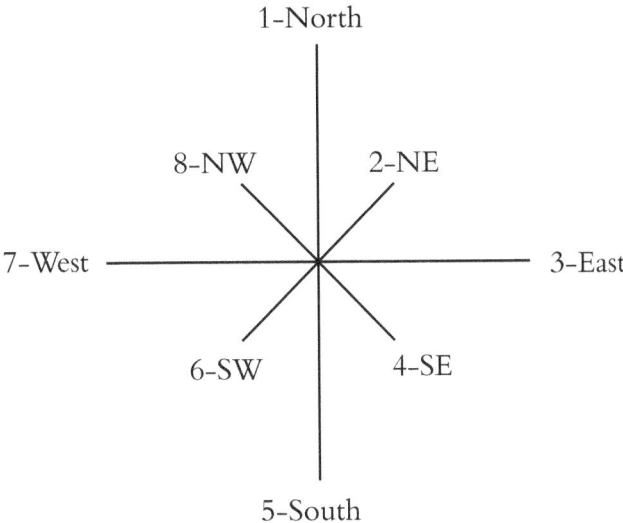

Figure 48.1 Compass points

Pupil 2: Our characters could easily get there in a day, so I think we need some obstacles.
Pupil 4: But wait, do our characters know about the treasure that the dragon's guarding?
Pupil 1: I'll flip the counter – no, they don't know.
Pupil 3: So why are they here? I think the treasure idea is a good one –
Pupil 2: They can find out about it later. We need a reason for them to be here now.
Pupil 1: Let's think of six reasons and roll the die to choose one – we can use the others another time.

The children came up with the following:

1. Searching for a magic crystal.
2. Tracking down an evil wizard.
3. Characters were sucked through a portal and need to get home.
4. Running from an invading army of orcs.
5. Searching for the final jewel to complete a 'chalice of power'.
6. Trying to find and save the world's last unicorn.

The dice roll gave number 3.

Pupil 4: So, sucked through a portal into this world.
Pupil 3: Depending on how the story grows, we may need to find out about the world our characters came from. But for now, you mentioned obstacles.

	Because we don't know about the treasure yet we might not be heading north, so we need dangers in other directions too. (Rolls eight-sided die) Four, so southeast.
Pupil 2:	Let's put something nearby. A swamp?
Pupil 4:	Shall we flip the counter?
Pupil 1:	I like the idea of a swamp. Can we just agree on it? (nods) I'll draw it in.
Pupil 3:	A haunted forest – or a forest with werewolves! (rolls eight-sided die) Six, so a forest in the southwest.
Pupil 1:	I can't wait to get in there and meet the werewolves!

As the children build their map you'll see that they are also working out the logic of the story, using a combination of random selection and discussion. Drawing and annotating the map as the story evolves also fits in with the principle of minimal writing (page 57). Less enthusiastic writers can still get involved with the story-making and will visualise the locations as vividly and with the same concentration as the others in the group.

The children here are creating a landscape (Figure 48.2), but the same 'dice journey' technique can be used to build maps of, for instance, a labyrinth of caves and tunnels in the mountains, a wizard's stronghold, a castle, a town, etc. And the technique can be combined with others we've described, such as 'sliderman' (page 142) and the use of a narrative line (page 100). There is also the opportunity here to introduce arithmetical concepts such as greater than, less than, farther from, numbers of and others.

Figure 48.2 Dice journey

Once the map is partially drawn, the children's characters can jump into the action. Shortly after the earlier discussion, the group decided that because a storm is coming and night is falling, the characters head into the forest for shelter without realising that it's plagued by werewolves. The decision has also been made that each child will be in control of one character.

Pupil 1: My character, Elyssa, scored four for magic. As we enter the darkness of the forest she makes her hands glow, so lighting the way.

Pupil 2: My character is Merion, brave but can be foolhardy. He's a good fighter but has not yet reached the peak of his skill. He walks beside Elyssa with his sword drawn.

Pupil 3: My character, Weland, is a hunter. In between distant booms of thunder, Weland can hear things moving stealthily in the undergrowth...

Pupil 1: And at the same time Elyssa notices the path stretching away into the trees – and then the gleam of many eyes reflecting the light from her hands.

Pupil 4: My character is Gorth and he's also a warrior. His weapon of choice is the longbow. As Elyssa shouts a warning, instinct makes Gorth turn around – only to see two fearsome werewolves running towards him. He puts an arrow into his bow, fires – I'll flip the counter to see if he hits one of the creatures. Yes.

Pupil 2: What's the injury score for the werewolf?

Pupil 4: (rolls six-sided die) Three, so the creature is only wounded. It howls in agony but keeps on coming, together with the second creature.

Pupil 2: Merion leaves Elyssa's side and hurries to join the fight.

Pupil 1: But the other werewolves are now charging towards the group. Elyssa can use her power to create a dazzling light from her hands but only for a short time until her energy is exhausted...

Once children get into the swing of the story the plot moves quickly. Any child can contribute as much or as little as he or she likes, though there is a certain 'positive pressure' to be involved as children usually want their characters to keep up with the others.

At this stage, no formal writing is being done. Advise groups to pause at appropriate moments and jot down in note form what has happened so far. This also gives them some thinking time to consider ideas about how the story might develop.

You may recognise that calculating distances, rolling dice for injury scores and so on are features of fantasy war gaming. Rules for this can be complicated and are beyond the scope of this book, though information is available online. Our experience has been that boys especially can become very interested in such gameplay, helping to develop their literacy, numeracy and social skills, as well as their imaginations.

Take it further:

- Invite groups to partially create a map, which is then passed on to another group for completion. Either group can then write the story set within the finished landscape.
- As well as children learning about geographical features in conjunction with map building, there is also an opportunity to familiarise them with Ordnance Survey map symbols if the story is set in the modern day. Should children want to set their story in the Arizona desert for example, that can form the basis of a research project so that there is some accuracy in imagining the location.
- Use children's maps as the basis for guided visualisations (page 73) and multisensory thinking (page 23 onwards).
- Children can enhance their maps with photographs of landscapes collected online, from magazines, etc.
- Maps can also be used as the locations featuring characters from children's favourite stories, or favourite characters from books can be set down in landscapes the children have created.

CHAPTER

Controlling the imagination

Do you remember the purple cat on page 32? Perhaps the child was just being silly or speaking impulsively when he said it. Explaining that the mind can pop up all kinds of ideas but that you have a choice over which you use helps children to 'rein in' their imaginations. A useful analogy is that the imagination is like a strong horse, 'but you are the rider and you have the reins. So you can run away with your imagination, but you wouldn't want that horse to gallop anywhere it wanted to'.

Here are a couple more techniques that children might find useful.

- Plastic money. Some children – more often boys – want to use excessive or gratuitous violence in their stories. If this is the case, give that person a few pounds' worth of plastic coins and tell him that any violence will cost, so he'll have to budget. You might have worked out a tariff for yourself earlier (mention of blood splattering 50p, decapitation £1.25, etc.) but it's also fun to haggle with the young writer as he figures out what he can afford to spend. This is also an opportunity for him to practise his mental arithmetic.
- Sliding scale. Consider doing this as a whole-class game. Ask the children to imagine a sliding scale of 1–5. One indicates ideas that are ordinary and everyday and/or explanations that are very reasonable and highly likely. Five indicates ideas that are weird and wonderful or explanations that are wacky and fantastical. So if a dog were frightening the cat, that idea would be a one on the scale. If it were being frightened by a green (or purple) alien from outer space, that would be a four or five.

The main purpose of this technique is to give children a measure of control over how they use their imagination. Sometimes stories are off-the-wall simply because the young writer can't think of anything else to put down, which suggests a failure of imagination rather than an indication of originality. Or maybe the child believes that incredible and outlandish tales are more entertaining. The sliding scale tool however gives them the increasing ability to choose where they pitch their ideas, allowing for greater flexibility in their work.

Here are other ways of using the sliding scale:

Creative linking. Refer to the linking game on page 110. Note down the various stories in a nutshell and then ask the children to place them along the 1–5 scale in terms of how reasonable or wacky the plot lines are.

Occam's razor. This is the notion in science that the simplest explanations are often the more likely ones. It is also known as the principle of economy or parsimony. Use the sliding scale technique in other subject areas. So for instance, show the class an experiment where liquid changes colour and ask them to provide possible explanations (that don't need to be 'right' or even scientific). Discuss where on the scale of 'reasonableness' any idea would fit – magic will always be a five! Take an event in history, such as the Great Fire of London or the construction of Stonehenge and, again, ask for possible explanations that range along the scale.

This simple game shows children how hypothesising works. A hypothesis is a possible working explanation based on a certain degree of evidence, sometimes very little. The hypothesis itself is the outcome of the creative linking of that evidence and gives direction for further questioning and the gathering of more information. Other thinking tools help to strengthen the children's ability to do this.

The three-step question technique. In order to strengthen a hypothesis ask the following:

a) What do we already know?
b) What do we think we know (i.e. our assumptions, speculations and inferences)?
c) What questions do we need to ask to find out more or to be sure?

If-then predictions. An important criterion for the accuracy or veracity of a hypothesis (or theory, which is what hypotheses evolve into as more evidence accumulates) is its predictive power. If the hypothesis is right, then it can be used to predict what will happen under certain circumstances. So placing a lighted candle in an opaque sealed container makes the flame go out after a short time. Ask the children what might account for this (assuming they don't already know). For each explanation, ask the class to come up with ways of testing it. For instance, if one tentative explanation is that the darkness inside the container causes the flame to go out, this can be tested by sealing the candle in a glass container to see what happens.

CHAPTER

Tackling text

The word 'text' shares its origins with context, textiles and texture, coming from the Latin 'to weave'. Pointing this out to children gives them a clear and concrete metaphor for putting words together. Writing text is the weaving up of ideas to create a fabric, one that has a pattern and a certain 'feel' to it – material that is, as it were, 'handmade' (which gives us a useful link to the word 'manuscript' meaning 'written by hand').

The kinds of thinking that you have cultivated in the children by exploring pictures to help them write their own stories and poems can also be used in a more analytical way when looking at other people's writing, both fiction and non-fiction. The approach to analysing any text is underpinned by the basic attitude of the following:

Being unafraid of ideas. Being ready, willing and able to question, challenge, doubt.

Understanding that the author will (usually) have written what he did and how he did for reasons he has thought about beforehand.

Realising on the children's part that the thinking they do will be valued by you.

Realising on your part that however basic, naïve or misinformed the children's analyses are, it is more useful to regard them as examples of emergent understanding rather than indicators of ignorance or being wrong. Also, since our aim is to help children to become more independent and sophisticated thinkers, even if their explanations are a bit shaky, they're better than simply parroting someone else's ideas and opinions.

During one workshop we ran a child asked, 'How many books have you writed?' Her teacher corrected her, but we also pointed out that she had grasped the concept of past tense. This is emergent understanding in action.

In terms of looking at fiction you can ask the children to do the following things, either as separate activities or in combination depending on the groups you're working with. We've put the activities in what we think is their order of

DOI: 10.4324/9781003184003-50

Tackling text

difficulty, although this is just our opinion and you or the children might disagree (challenge, question, doubt)!

Use our story 'A Muddy Road' or choose one of your own.

> A Muddy Road.
>
> Once there were two monks coming home from market. Their names were Tanzan and Ekido. They were making their way to the monastery in the hills. It had been raining. The ground was very muddy and the streams were full and fast flowing.
>
> As Tanzan and Ekido came around a bend they saw a young woman struggling with her shopping baskets. She was trying to cross a ford but was worried about getting her sandals and the hem of her kimono soaking wet.
>
> 'I'll help you,' Tanzan said with a smile. He lifted the girl in his arms and carried her across the water and then returned for her baskets. The girl smiled in return and thanked him, and they all went on their way.
>
> Ekido was clearly angered by what had happened, for no monk was supposed to have anything to do with women. His temper increased until, as they approached the monastery, he could not hold himself back any longer. 'Why did you help that girl, Tanzan?' he raged. 'You know the rules of our monastery!'
>
> 'Oh,' Tanzan said calmly. 'I see you are still carrying the lady, while I put her down at the ford'.

When looking at stories and poems children can –

a) Underline or note words or sentences you don't understand. You can research them later.
b) Do a 'VAK scan'. This means the following:

If the writer helps you to see a picture and/or colour in your mind, put a V (for visual) near that word or sentence.

If the author helps you to hear a sound in your imagination, put an A (for auditory) close by.

If the writer helps you to have an emotion or imagine a physical sensation, put a K (for kinaesthetic [physical] near that word or sentence).

c) Notice your own thoughts. Most writers will help you to see pictures, hear sounds and have feelings/sensations. Notice the sentences that give you that kind of rich mental experience.
d) Play with certain sentences. Change some of the words. What effect does that have on the meaning of a sentence or how you or your friends imagine it?
e) 'Jump into' the story and be one of the characters. Or you can be yourself standing there in that landscape. What other things do you notice about it now?

f) The writer will probably have written the story or poem very deliberately, choosing what she'd like you to imagine for good reasons. Find some examples of the author's particular use of language – certain words or the way a sentence has been written for example – and suggest the reason(s) the writer might have had in mind.

g) Play the game called 'What do I know, what do I think I know?' This means that the author will give us certain information that helps us to work out other things. For example, where might the story be set? Why might Ekido have been so angry that Tanzan helped the girl across the ford, even though no one at the monastery need ever know?

h) Make up your own comprehension questions about the story or poem. These can be based on the things that have puzzled you (and maybe still do). Or you might understand the writing very well. In that case, make a list of questions for someone who is only just beginning to understand what it's about.

i) Working with friends, create a list of 'I think . . . because. . .' statements. See the following for example:

I think the story happens long ago because. . .

I think Tanzan is younger than Ekido because. . .

I think the two monks were walking home rather than riding on horses because . . .

CHAPTER

Thoughts, feelings, memories and dreams

The underpinning focus of this book is to enable children to have more control over their thoughts, not just what they think but also how they think. Our minds are constantly active. Throughout the day pictures and other thoughts stream through our heads; some of these we notice while others are peripheral, though all have the potential to influence our behaviour. At night when we are 'un-conscious' (when our conscious awareness is absent), subconsciously we are assimilating the day's events and embedding our experiences into a kind of mental map of what we think the world is like and how we fit into it. This metaphor is sometimes called the 'map of reality', although like any map it's not the territory itself, but rather a representation of the sense we have made so far of our life experiences. Thus, although we might agree that a table is a table (consensus reality) the network of personal associations attached to the concept of a table will most likely be unique to each of us.

Because our thoughts, feelings, physiology and behaviour are interconnected, the ability to notice and manipulate our thoughts becomes important in the field of emotional resourcefulness. This is a large and fascinating subject supported by vast literature. It is beyond the scope of this book to delve very deeply into the subject, but given what your children will hopefully have learned about visualising and using their imagination so far, we'll touch on some techniques that have proved particularly effective and beneficial.

CHAPTER

Mindfulness

Mindfulness is the experience of being aware of and fully within the present moment rather than lost in memories or thoughts of the future, with all their attendant emotions. At its most basic it consists of the focussing of one's attention, usually beginning by noticing the breath (a very calming activity in itself), followed by really looking at an object, really listening to sounds and so on. The next step is to be aware of one's thoughts and feelings without getting lost in them or trying to modify them; simply letting them come and go.

The key to developing mindfulness is regularity of practice, beginning with a few minutes each day of noticing the breath before moving on to giving attention to objects and then to thoughts. While becoming more mindful complements many of the visualisation activities in this book (while they in turn help to develop mindfulness), there are other reasons for teaching the technique to the children:

Mindfulness reduces stress.
It improves concentration and focus.
It creates a quiet time during a busy day.
It enhances appreciation of things: ordinary objects, people we meet, small experiences.
It develops emotional resourcefulness: the ability to notice, distinguish and modify our feelings.

Joanne O'Malley (see the Mindfulness at Work weblink) asserts that neuroscientific research has found that training in mindfulness allows a person to be clearer in their thinking, calmer, more focussed, more creative 'and even more compassionate', insofar as it leads to a non-judgemental awareness, a direct knowing of what is going on inside of us moment by moment (see also 'obserpinions' on page 18).

As a preliminary activity in mindfulness, ask the children to sit upright but not rigid on their chairs. They can close their eyes or keep them open. Then do the following:–

Breathe in to a slow count of six, noticing the air entering the body.
Hold the breath for a count of two.
Breathe out slowly to a count of six, noticing the air leaving the lungs.
Hold for a count of two.
Repeat five or six times.

The process takes just a couple of minutes, but the calming effects will be immediate for many of the children and will be cumulative if practised daily.

For more on mindfulness see, for example, Bowkett (2017); Doyle (2014); Han (2014).

Related activities follow in the next chapter.

CHAPTER

A special place

Ask the children to settle themselves and relax and then begin gathering their thoughts to create an impression of a place that's pleasant and comfortable, a place they can enjoy. This might be an actual place that they have visited, seen pictures of or read about, or it can be somewhere entirely imaginary, possibly a place taken from a story. Encourage multisensory thinking within the visualisations and for children to notice some details that make the place their own. It's important that this setting evokes pleasant feelings, whatever they may be.

Another vital point is that *each place is that child's own*. As such, she or he does not have to tell anyone else about it (though can if she or he chooses to). Explain these points to the class before gently guiding them into making the most of the session. Here's a suggested script for doing this:

'Even before beginning to imagine your special place, think back to some pleasant times when you felt very positive, happy, amused, safe – or any other good feelings that come to you. Notice how those feelings express themselves in your body and let them stay there. That's why they're called feelings; you feel them in your nerves and muscles and organs. Enjoy those good feelings all over again.

'Now, gather up your thoughts to create your special place. You can notice the colours you find there, picking out those distinct and separate colours in this place where you imagine yourself to be. (Pause.) And you can be aware of the sounds you find there, becoming more aware of those clear and quite distinctive sounds. (Pause.) And if you want to, you can reach out and feel the surfaces and textures of things in this place that you're thinking about. (Pause.)

'And I don't know if you're thinking of somewhere that's well known and familiar to you, or if you're creating a place that's quite new and wonderfully different. But whatever you're doing, you can enjoy this place even more by noticing new and interesting details. And even as you notice these, you remember those pleasant feelings all over again and realise that whenever you visit this place, these lovely feelings will be there waiting for you'.

Notice how the guidelines are artfully vague and adhere to the principle of flexibility within a structure. You are offering enough information to give the children a definite how-to technique, yet leaving sufficient creative space for each child to imagine her or his own unique location, a kind of verbal join-the-dots where children complete the picture for themselves. Notice too how the script emphasises the link between what the child imagines and the pleasant feelings that accompany the image. In effect you are creating a positive anchor between the imagined place and the bundle of good feelings so that the more a child visits her or his special place, even just for several seconds, that mental act will evoke the associated feelings. This is the literal meaning of remembering – 're-membering', bringing back into the members (parts of the body) feelings and emotions previously experienced.

Here are a few other tips:

Never *insist* that a child do this visualisation.

If anyone would prefer not to, their wish must be respected. If any unpleasant thoughts/feelings arise, advise children beforehand that they can simply open their eyes and take their minds off the feelings by reading a book, watching a video, etc.

Once the pleasant place has been established, suggest that children can add an extra detail or two each time they go there. John, a friend of ours, imagines a bamboo hut on top of a hill overlooking an extensive forest. Inside the hut a log fire is burning, the flames giving out a cosy golden light. To the left by the wall of the hut stands an old bookcase. On the shelves are some cherished books, ornaments and toys. John still owns some of these in reality, though others vanished long ago and are 'just' memories. Each time he goes to his special place he puts another treasured possession on the shelf. Sometimes the memory of a toy or book comes to him spontaneously once his intention to revisit his special place is clear.

Every now and then, choose a good feeling that the children can add to their treasure chest of positive emotions. You may want to discuss your choice with the class beforehand. During one workshop the class discussed what wonder felt like and the kinds of things that could evoke such an emotion. Subsequently during the visualisation, John stepped out of his hut. It was evening and the sky beyond the forest blazed with the colours of sunset. As the darkness deepened, *two* moons rose over the roof of the hut. Following this, the stars came out and John imagined the Milky Way arching across the sky but as though seen from much closer to the centre of the galaxy (look at some long exposure photographs of the heavens to get a sense of this). His interest in astronomy and science fiction primed him to choose this imagery to evoke a sense of wonder.

This raises the point of how to deal with children who have limited life experiences. It's a difficult issue since as teachers we have little influence over our pupils' home lives. On the other hand, surely a central aim of education is to enrich children's experience as much as we can in as many ways as possible. One powerful way is by developing and nourishing the imagination through books, comics, videos and so on that are both fictional and factual, bearing in mind that an imagined experience can be as powerful as a 'real' one. This is why, in our view, the humanities need to be as important a part of the curriculum as the sciences.

Another addition to an imagined special place is the 'helpful friend'. This is a figure who can be invited into a child's domain, just for company or to sit and listen, or to offer useful advice. (This last idea is based on the principle that we subconsciously know more than we consciously do.) So for instance, a child is able to write a story because of all the other narratives he has experienced so far in his life. Details of these stories are, so to speak, written down on his map of reality and may then be forgotten[1], but during the creative flow, snippets of tales or entire stories 'pop into mind'. That is to say, they are recalled (called back into conscious awareness) and remembered (i.e. the feelings associated with those tales are experienced all over again).

Creative activities tend to 'open the doors' a little more to our subconscious resources, which is why ideas flow with little or no effort when we're in a creative mood.

The helpful friend could be a cartoon character, a superhero, a character from a favourite story or an actual person such as a historical figure or someone currently in the news. Once a child invites the friend into the special place (i.e. makes a conscious decision to do so), a subconscious search is activated so that scraps and fragments about that character are gathered up and brought to conscious awareness. Note though that like the other visualisation activities in this book, practice develops this particular skill so that it works more effectively over time.

A friend might be helpful simply by sharing the mental space with the child, keeping her company. Or the child may be looking for an insight[2], perhaps a specific piece of advice. In that case, it's useful if the child clearly articulates the problem – maybe writing it down beforehand – and then frames the clear intention that advice will be forthcoming. Again this is based on the principle of 'we know more than we think we know'.

Along the road. The same developing ability to visualise also enables us to envisage possible futures for ourselves. While it's true that in a series of well-known movies we are told that 'the future is not set', our imaginations allow us to look ahead in time to what might be. Underpinning this again is the notion of forming a clear intention of what we would like to achieve. The word 'intend' comes from the Middle English *entend*, 'to direct the attention to', itself deriving from the Latin *intendere*, from *in-* 'towards' and *tendere* 'stretch, tend'. So an intention gives us – through a 'stretch' of the imagination – a sense of direction supported by the motivation to follow that path.

Imagining a desired future primes us at different levels to realise the vision, 'to make it real in one's life', while our emotions supply the driving force – the word emotion meaning to excite and to move. Various sages have urged us to 'follow your dreams', leading us to make the obvious point that we need to have the dream before we have something to follow. The internationally renowned mythologist Joseph Campbell put it even more strongly when he advised his students to 'follow your bliss' (Campbell (1988)), adding to that the story of a successful businessman who climbed the ladder of material success, only to discover towards the end of his life that he'd put his ladder against the wrong wall.

(For Campbell, myths were powerful sources of guidance, archetypal stories containing deep truths. He felt that many of our problems, especially in the West, arose because the cultures had become 'demythologised'. Significantly, he was consulted by George Lucas, creator of the Star Wars universe, who through those films wanted to build 'a myth for the twentieth century'. See Campbell (1988); Boa (1989); Larsen (1990).)

Body scan. This is a simple but powerful visualisation/relaxation technique. Ask the children to sit comfortably on their seats, eyes open or closed. If open, children should rest their gaze on a point on the wall at eye level and not be distracted by other things in the room.

'Imagine a gentle, flat plane of light hovering above your head. Give the light a colour you like. Imagine too that as the light passes down through your body, it both relaxes you and gathers up your energy for the rest of the day.

'Let the light sink slowly down through yourself. As it passes by your forehead, if you are frowning let the frown fade. (Pause.) As it passes down your face, let your face muscles relax. (Pause.) Now let the light sink through your shoulders, letting them relax. (Pause.) Keep imagining the light sinking slowly down through you, relaxing your chest, stomach, legs, etc. Take what time you need, and when the light reaches your feet it fades away, leaving your whole body relaxed but energised'.

Tip: The time children take to go through this process will vary. Suggest that once a child finishes the visualisation, she or he can perhaps read or simply sit and enjoy the sense of relaxation and peace until everyone has finished. Or the child can run the body scan again.

Energy boost. Again ask children to sit comfortably, eyes open or closed.

'Put your point of attention at the base of your spine. Imagine that just there is a ball of energy. It's your energy, like a treasure that you didn't know you had until now. You might imagine the energy as a lovely warmth or as a really nice shimmering feeling or some other pleasant sensation. When you are ready, let the ball of energy expand all through you, down through your legs and rising up through your stomach and chest, arms and head until your whole self feels bathed in the energy, which will give you a boost to help you through the day'.

Tip: Unlike the body scan visualisation, the energy boost usually happens quickly. We experience it as a kind of tingling surge, an uplifting feeling rising from the bottom of the spine, through the body and head. It's a subjective thing, so children will report different sensations (or maybe nothing at all). If you run this activity from time to time, those children who do feel a rise of energy will probably be able to make it happen whenever they wish, even as they're walking along, talking with friends and so on.

Thanking yourself. Through strengthening the imagination in the ways we've been exploring, many children will come to develop a more refined appreciation of the things around them. They may notice the great range of greens during a walk in the park, the unique shape of every tree, the particular way leaves tremble in a breeze. They may wonder more often at the amazing creativity of the human mind that has produced so many incredible things which could be so easy to take for granted (as many people do). In short, strengthening the imagination makes the world a richer, more varied, more exciting and amazing place.

That same sense of appreciation and wonder can be extended to oneself. For instance, according to wonderopolis.org, there are around 37 trillion cells in the human body, while the brain is composed of about 100 billion cells, each cell connecting up with tens of thousands of others, allowing the mind to express itself. For comparison, just one trillion grains of sand would occupy a space of 65 cubic metres (Ref: Quora.com).

Although, unfortunately, many people struggle with a range of physical difficulties, the way that number of cells work together to allow us to experience life is astounding. With this in mind, we feel it is not at all strange to thank oneself for the fact of one's own existence and the opportunity of life. Similarly, when we have a new idea or when a name that we want to remember pops into mind, thanking oneself does not seem in any way odd. Because thoughts, feelings and physiology are connected, all part of the whole that is a person, these acts of 'self-thanking' will have a cumulative and beneficial effect.

Ask children to imagine looking at themselves in the mirror. As they do, ask them to reflect (pun intended) on what a unique and wonderful creation they are. Allow them to appreciate themselves in whatever way they choose – mentally saying thank you, noticing a smile from their reflected image, or a friendly wave of the hand or a simple but important realisation that 'this is me at this particular point in my life'.

Self-stories. Patterns of thoughts-feelings-behaviours are established in childhood and laid down in the mind as 'narratives', stories we tell ourselves that in the field of transactional analysis are called life scripts or childhood stories. These are built up through children's interaction with peers, parents, teachers and other adults and, increasingly, messages put out by the media. It's well-known that such messages can lead to anxiety and stress, especially so in children whose relatively limited mental resources and experience of the world mean that sometimes they don't have the wherewithal to reflect on *and change* their worldview and self-image (Ref: www.psychologytoday.com 'The Anxious Stories We Tell Ourselves').

Childhood stories are almost invariably accompanied by mental images and sounds: of self, of remembered and constructed scenes from the news, etc. The tendency is for these scenes to be remembered in the same way each time, but the important points to note here are the following:

The scenes themselves (from a news report or created in the imagination from something someone has said or whatever) represent just one point of view and, in the case of the media, a highly edited fragment of the event.

More broadly, the news from whatever source amounts to choices programme makers have made about what 'the public' should see and hear with regard to what's going on in the world. Millions of events happen daily worldwide, so what we get is a tiny selection put together to convey a particular worldview (see De Botton (2014)).

We have the potential to *reconstruct* our mental images such that we can change the way we feel as we experience these memories, eventually and with practice influencing aspects of the life scripts that pass through our minds.

The mental images and stories we run and rerun in our minds need not just be memories. We also have the capacity to construct imagined future scenarios, which, if they are negative, can cause us to worry ahead of time, regardless of the likelihood of any particular scenario actually happening. The field of emotional resourcefulness is large and fascinating and supported by a huge literature. There are scores of techniques for increasing one's ability to develop the way we think to help dampen 'negative self-talk' and so begin to rewrite life scripts which may be having an adverse effect – see, for instance, Bowkett (2017), Carnegie (1972), Day (1994), and Markham (1991).

Dale Carnegie's *How to Stop Worrying and Start Living* was invaluable through Steve's teens, when he was a great worrier. The book is full of uplifting anecdotes, practical advice and powerful strategies for dealing with anxiety and the habits of thought that underpin it. Eventually, the copy cited in the 'References and Resources' section – which Steve still has on his bookshelf – became a positive kinaesthetic anchor: just holding the book dampens worry and replaces it with feelings of optimism and calmness.

Anchoring and visualisation can be combined. Dr Roger Jones in his book *Physics as Metaphor* (Jones (1983)) recounts the time when, as a child, he watched the Alexander Korda film *The Thief of Bagdad* and was fascinated by a magical ruby called the all-seeing eye which appeared in the story. Subsequent recollections of the jewel evoked all over again the magical visions, the exotic Arabian culture and the romantic adventures, all of which added vibrant colour and meaning to the 'bare memory of the ruby, and (made) it dazzle all the more within my mind'. So simply remembering a special object can bring forward a raft of memories and the good feelings that accompany them.

There is not room here to do more than scratch the surface when it comes to using the imagination to influence one's feelings. Following up on some of the references will give you directions for exploring further. Here however are a few more simple techniques that have proved effective:

Sombunall. The writer and philosopher Robert Anton Wilson coined this term (Wilson (1999)). It means 'some but not all'. It is a powerful counter to any tendency to generalise or automatically buy into a worse-case scenario. So 'the world today is a more dangerous place than it was 50 years ago'. (Some but not all parts of the world are more dangerous some, but not all of the time, than they were 50 years ago'.) 'Young children are coming to school who are not toilet trained'. (Some but not all young children are coming to school who are not toilet trained'.)

Maybe thinking (see page 16). 'Maybe' is as useful as 'sombunall' for opening up one's perspective, highlighting further options and countering unwanted negative feelings. 'Kids in my class laughed as I walked by earlier. They're making fun of me. I feel terrible'. Maybe one of them has just told a joke. Maybe they are laughing at somebody else or at each other. Maybe they are talking about a comedy movie they'd watched. Maybe they haven't even noticed me going by.

The positive opposite. Thinking the positive opposite of a negative thought helps to neutralise the unwanted feelings that accompany it and dampens the tendency to rerun the negative thought again and again. So, 'I won't do well in my test – I will do well in my test', etc. If the negative thought persists after repeatedly countering it with the positive opposite, select other techniques to support it, perhaps ones from this book or others contained in recommendations we've made in the references section. Life coaching strategies are also powerful for developing one's imagination and thinking skills to effect positive change – see for instance Bowkett and Percival (2011); Harrold (2000); Preston (2006).

The bigger picture. The media filter news such that it can seem the world is full of tragedy, suffering and horror. But realistically, for every disturbing news story we encounter, there are thousands of stories of hope, kindness and joy that we never see. In making this point to children, show them a picture of Earth seen from space and ask them to visualise this each time they experience unwanted feelings arising from what they've read in the news. Accompany this by actively seeking out positive stories in the media.

Future self. Visualise yourself at some chosen point in the future when you have gained more experience of the world, have learned more, have a more mature attitude towards life. The visualisation doesn't need to be detailed in terms of how you look: you may just have an uplifting sense of being more confident and capable. If you find this technique helpful, ask future-you to keep giving you positive feelings and even some specific advice.

What would my hero do? Pick a character you admire from a book, comic or film. Put that character in a situation you want to change. What would that character do? Obviously, if your hero has superpowers and uses them, you can't do the same thing. But what qualities does the character reveal – patience, determination, relying on others to help?

Worry dolls. These are tiny figures made in Guatemala. According to legend, Guatemalan children tell each doll about one of their worries and then put the dolls under the pillow before going to sleep, reminding themselves that by the morning the dolls will have taken the worries away.

Worry envelope. Write your worries on a piece of paper and put them in the envelope, together with a date several weeks or months in the future. When that date arrives, open the envelope. You may be surprised to realise that the problems you noted down never happened, or that you've dealt with them or that you forgot about them entirely. The writer Mark Twain said, 'I've had many worries in my life, most of which never happened'. (This epithet has also been attributed to Winston Churchill.)

The wheatfield. Imagine your mind as a field of ripe wheat, shimmering in the sun on a summer's day. If you walk across the field, you will leave a faint track. Walk the same path and the track will become more obvious. If you keep following that path it will become fully established as a habit of thought.

To make this visualisation work you need to practise regularly. If you have a habit of thought that you don't like, such as worrying or low self-confidence, imagine it as a track that you've walked along in the past without really wanting or intending to. Now choose a different direction so that you can make a new path, towards feeling calm and confident for instance. Deliberately ignore the old pathway. It won't be long before the wheat grows over it and it will disappear. The more you walk the new path, the more you can experience the positive thoughts and feelings that you desire.

Note: Because the mind and body are linked, people who have a pollen or dust allergy can react physically to the mental image of a wheatfield[3]. If any child shows the slightest sign of this, get her to change the imagery, to wet sand on a beach or a pleasant street or just tracing a different path on an imagined map.

Think in metaphors. The wheatfield is a metaphor: it represents or stands for an instruction you give to yourself to change direction and move towards a place in your thoughts and feelings where you'd rather be. The worry dolls are also metaphors, acting as symbols that you pass your worries on to.

There are hundreds of things you can use as a metaphor to change the way you think, feel and behave:

A flower can represent the way you'll flourish in the future.
A rock is what you stand on to feel confident and strong.
A path marks the direction you choose to move in.
Clouds can stand for the idea that problems come and go.
A tree can symbolise the idea that often there are many branches you can choose from.
Scatter your worries on a stream like leaves and watch them float away.

What other objects can children think of that might be turned into helpful metaphors?

A gift for a friend. If a visualisation has worked well for you, offer it as a gift for a friend. Either write it out so that your friend can use it whenever she wants to or sit with your friend and guide her through it. Doing this occasionally is a way of strengthening friendships and creating a 'community of good thinkers' in the classroom.

Note: In her book *Creative Visualisation With Children*, Jennifer Day (Day (1994)) offers a structure for running visualisations. Aspects include creative movement, breathing exercises, centring and meditation techniques as preparation for the visualisation itself. In an ideal world there would be time in a school day to go through the whole routine, but we realise that practically speaking the time will not be available. In that case, ask the children simply to settle themselves and relax, taking a few deep breaths before concentrating on the chosen visualisation.

A related point is that *the mind works quickly*. An unwanted negative thought can appear in a moment, together with its associated unwanted feelings. By the same token, positive thoughts and feelings can be evoked in seconds, especially if children have practised some of the other techniques in this book (such as multisensory thinking) and have developed the ability to focus, concentrate and pack plenty of detail into their imagined scenarios.

Notes

1. The etymology of the word is interesting, and we think misleading. According to etymonline.com the word derives from the Old English *forgietan*, in the sense of to 'un-get' or to lose from one's mind. We would argue that a forgotten piece of information is not at that moment present in conscious awareness but may well be stored at a subconscious level. So for instance we've probably all tried to remember a name and experienced that tip-of-the-tongue feeling. Trying to remember usually doesn't work, and the harder we try the more elusive and distant the name seems to be. But if we let it go and suggest to ourselves that 'it'll come to me', often it does quite spontaneously and with no effort involved. Beforehand the name was forgotten but not lost to the mind.
2. This word suggests 'looking in' or rather drawing upon our subconscious resources. It's closely linked to the idea of intuition – by this we mean 'inner tuition', being advised and guided by the mental/emotional resources we have available at that point in our lives.
3. Many years ago Steve qualified as a hypnotherapist. During training his tutor, David, told the class that he'd once dealt with a client who presented with a pollen allergy. After he'd explained what hypnotherapy entailed, the client remained skeptical that 'just talking and thinking' could influence physical symptoms. However, she agreed to have a first session. When she arrived, David opened the door to his treatment room for her to enter first. The client was horrified to see a vase of flowers on a nearby coffee table and immediately reacted with sneezing, itchy eyes, runny nose and the rest. David said, 'Oh, I'm sorry if you don't like these plastic flowers. Let me take them away for you'. Such is the power of the mind!

CHAPTER

Imagination beyond the curriculum

We hope that the techniques we've explained will quickly bring benefits to the way children think, feel and behave with regard to their learning. But developing the imagination and boosting its creative power is also a life skill. In the same way that in stories we will always need heroes to resolve[1] problems, so we will always need creative people to come up with effective solutions to the problems that will inevitably arise in an ever-changing and increasingly complex world.

As we were writing this book there was much in the news about reducing carbon emissions, cutting back on plastic use and related environmental crises. The point came up often that these are problems we need to address now rather than leaving them for future generations to tackle. It's an important insight, though an obvious one, that short-termism or acting ineffectually or doing nothing is morally wrong, especially if as educators we fail to equip our children with the mental wherewithal to try and put right what previous generations failed to rectify. But we *can* equip them, using the techniques we've explored, plus others, to strengthen what the psychologist Stephen Larsen calls the 'wondrous world-building faculty' of imagination (Larsen (1990)).

With that in mind, we began with a quote from Albert Einstein and would like to end with one:

'Logic will get you from A to Z; imagination will get you everywhere'.

Note

1. Resolve means to 're-solve', to solve again. This reading of the word highlights the fact that humankind will always have its problems, villains and heroes. The idea of a resolution in a story echoes this.

References and resources

Note: Publication dates of books refer to the editions we used in our research. All website links were active at the time of writing.

Baldwin, P. *With drama in mind*. London: Continuum, 2003.
Baldwin, P. & Fleming, K. *Teaching literacy through drama: Creative approaches*. London: Routledge Farmer, 2003.
Barrow, R. *Understanding skills: Thinking, feeling and caring*. London: The Althouse Press, 1990.
Berger, W. *A more beautiful question*. New York: Bloomsbury, 2014.
Boa, F. *The way of myth: Talking with Joseph Campbell*. Boston, MA: Shambala, 1989.
Bowkett, S. *Developing self-confidence in young writers*. London: Bloomsbury, 2017.
Bowkett, S. *Jumpstart! Philosophy in the classroom*. Abingdon, Oxon: Routledge, 2018.
Bowkett, S. & Hitchman, T. *Using comic art to improve speaking, reading and writing*. Abingdon, Oxon: Routledge, 2012.
Bowkett, S. & Hogston, K. *Jumpstart! Wellbeing*. Abingdon, Oxon: Routledge, 2017.
Bowkett, S. & Percival, S. *Coaching emotional intelligence in the classroom*. Abingdon, Oxon: Routledge, 2011.
Browning Wroe, J. & Lambert, D. *Visual literacy book 1*. Hyde, Cheshire: LDA (Learn Develop Achieve), 2008.
Buckley, J. *Pocket P4C: Getting started with philosophy for children*. Chelmsford: One Slice Books, 2011.
Campbell, J. *The power of myth*. New York: Doubleday, 1988.
Carnegie, D. *How to stop worrying and start living*. Bungay, Suffolk: World's Work Ltd., 1972.
Clarke, A. C. *Greetings, carbon-based bipeds!* London: HarperCollins, 1999a.
Clarke, A. C. *Profiles of the future: An inquiry into the limits of the possible*. London: Orion, 1999b.
Cohen, M. *101 ethical dilemmas*. London: Routledge, 2003.
Day, J. *Creative visualization with children*. Shaftsbury, Dorset: Element, 1994.

De Botton, A. *The news: A user's manual*. London: Hamish Hamilton, 2014.

Dilts, R. & Epstein, T. A. *Dynamic learning*. Capitola, CA: Meta Publications, 1995.

Doyle, O. *Mindfulness plain & simple*. London: Orion, 2014.

Egan, K. *Imagination in teaching and learning: Ages 8-15*. London: Routledge, 2002.

Fontana, D. & Slack, I. *Teaching meditation to children*. Shaftsbury, Dorset: Element, 1997.

Habgood, J. *Varieties of unbelief*. London: Darton, Longman & Todd, 2000.

Hanh, T. N. *How to sit*. Berkeley, CA: Parallax Press, 2014.

Harrold, F. *Be your own life coach*. London: Hodder & Stoughton, 2000.

Jones, R. *Physics as metaphor*. London: Abacus, 1983.

Langrehr, J. *Learn to think: Basic exercises in the core thinking skills for ages 6-11*. Abingdon, Oxon: Routledge, 2008.

Larsen, S. *The mythic imagination*. New York: Bantam Books, 1990.

Laws, S. *The philosophy files/the philosophy files 2*. London: Orion, 2002, 2006.

Magnus, M. *Gods in the word*. CreateSpace Independent Publishing Platform, 2010 (ISBN 9781453824443).

Markham, U. *The elements of visualisation*. Shaftsbury, Dorset: Element Books, 1991.

McGuinness, D. *Why children can't read: And what we can do about it*. London: Penguin, 1998.

Mitchell, J. *Euphonics: A poet's dictionary of enchantments*. Glastonbury: Wooden Books, 2006.

Nagel, T. *What does it all mean?* Oxford: Oxford University Press, 1987.

O'Connor, J. & Seymour, J. *Introducing neuro-linguistic programming*. London: Mandala, 1990.

Ozaniec, N. *Everyday meditation (101 essential tips)*. London: Dorling Kindersley, 1997.

Postman, N. & Weingartner, C. *Teaching as a subversive activity*. Harmondsworth, England: Penguin, 1971.

Preston, D. L. *365 Ways to be your own life coach*. Oxford: How to Books, 2006.

Rockett, M. & Percival, S. *Thinking for learning*. Stafford: Network Educational Press, 2002.

Rosenthal, R. & Jacobson, L. *Pygmalion in the classroom: Teacher expectation and pupils' intellectual development*. Bancyfelin, Wales: Crown House, 2003.

Rowshan, A. *Telling tales: How to help children deal with the challenges of life*. Oxford: One World, 1997.

Sacks, D. *The alphabet*. London: Hutchinson, 2003.

Schneiderman, K. *Step out of your story: Writing your way to the life you want: Writing exercises to reframe and transform your life*. Novato, CA: New World Library, 2015.

Stafford, T. *Teaching visual literacy in the primary classroom*. Abingdon, Oxon: Routledge, 2011.

Stock, G. *The kids' book of questions*. New York: Workman, 2004.

Sunderland, M. *Using story telling as a therapeutic tool with children*. Bicester, Oxon: Winslow Press, 2000.

Von Petzinger, G. *The first signs*. New York: Atria (Simon & Schuster), 2016.
Wallas, L. *Stories for the third ear*. London: W. W. Norton & Co., 1985.
William, T. *Mind games: 25 thought experiments to ignite your imagination*. USA: Zaze & Drury Publishing House, 2015.
Wilson, R. A. *The new inquisition*. Phoenix, Arizona: New Falcon Publications, 1999.

Note: The following websites are listed in the order in which they are referenced in the text.

http://truthdive.com/2013/03/29/Kids-ask-mums-nearly-300-questions-a-day/
https://worddreams.wordpress.com/2015/04/06/118-ways-to-describe-sound/
https://sportsandthemind.com/sport-perfomance-imagination/
https://faculty.washington.edu/chudler/syne.html
https://literarydevices.net/synesthesia/
https://www.brainpickings.org/2012/08/20/mars-and-the-mind-of-man-sagan-bradbury-clarke-caltech-1971/
https://www.stanford.edu/search/?q=Plato
https://warwick.ac.uk/fac/cross_fac/iatl/activities/modules/ugmodules/human-animalstudies/lectures/32/nagel_bat.pdf
https://kathysteinemann.com/Musings/colors/
https://plato.stanford.edu/entries/thought-experiment/
https://www.livescience.com/33179-does-human-body-replace-cells-seven-years.html
https://www.wordclouds.com/
https://www.closertotruth.com/series/does-evil-disprove-god
https://en.wiktionary.org/wiki/logo
https://conversations.marketing-partners.com/2013/03/logo-design-101-the-symbol/
https://www.thoughtco.com/geometric-shapes-4086370
http://history-world.org/hieroglyphics.htm
https://en.oxforddictionaries.com/explore/how-many-words-are-there-in-the-english-language/
https://www.thoughtco.com/phonestheme-word-sounds-1691505
https://discoveringegypt.com/egyptian-hieroglyphic-writing/hieroglyphic-typewriter/
https://www.penn.museum/cgi/hieroglyphsreal.php
https://www.kidzone.ws/cultures/egypt/hieroglyph.htm
https://assets.publishing.service.gov.uk/government/uploads/system/uploads/attachment_data/file/190599/Letters_and_Sounds_-_DFES-00281-2007.pdf
https://www.dyslexia-reading-well.com/support-files/the-44-phonemes-of-english.pdf
https://wonderopolis.org/wonder/how-many-cells-are-in-the-human-body
https://www.quora.com/What-does-one-trillion-grains-of-sand-look-like

References and resources

www.psychologytoday.com 'The Anxious Stories We Tell Ourselves'
https://mindfulnessatwork.ie
https:///www.psychologytoday.com/us/blog/the-stories-we-tell-ourselves/201507/the-anxious-stories-we-tell-ourselves

Index

abduction (inference to the best explanation) 15
abstract nouns 123
abstract shapes 133
alliteration 33, 118
anchoring 11, 114
artful vagueness 57
associating, of letters 130
assumed knowledge 51
auditory thinking 35, 54
author intention 149

bare bones writing 88
'because' used in reasoning 13
blackout poetry 58
brainstorming 114

chain stories 58
character creation 67
cliché 31, 35
closed questions 145
conditional (would-be) thinking 27
connotations 118
conventions of a genre 4, 68
convergent thinking and closed questions 144
creativity, stages of 88
criteria of quality in language 30

daydreaming 3
differentiation by outcome 5
divergent thinking 144

Egan, Kieran (educationist) 2, 3
Einstein, Albert 91
emergent understanding 157
emotional resourcefulness 160

enquiry method of education 2, 17
euphony (pleasing sounds) 33, 118

flexibility within a structure as a teaching strategy 57

generativity of language 126
guided visualisation 73

hypothesising 156

idea 1, 3
if-then thinking 18
imagination, controlling 155
inferential thinking 13
insight 88, 165
instructional writing 84
intuition 165

jumping to conclusions 13

kinaesthetic thinking 41

life scripts 103
logical consistency in narrative 81, 144

map of reality metaphor 160
'maybe hand' for speculating 16
meditation 10, 37
metacognition (noticing and manipulating one's thoughts) 3
metaphor 10, 27, 157
micro poems 60
minimal writing strategy 57
minisagas 57
modelling the behaviour 8

Index

mood gallery 120
motifs 22
motivation 166
'Muddy Road, A' 158
multisensory thinking 41
'muttering the understanding' 35
myth 166

neuro linguistic programming (NLP) 69

Occam's Razor (principle of parsimony) 156
onomatopoeia 37
originality 4
ownership of language 38

paradox 95
pathetic fallacy 63
paying attention 9
perceptual positions 69
phonaestheme 130
phonemic awareness 37
predicting 91
presupposition of success using 'when' 27
principle of utilisation (turning a possible negative into a positive) 12
prompted visualisation 72

question analysis 21, 149
quick feedback 8

randomness in creativity, using two-colour counters and dice 146
repetition 60, 118, 120
research skills 17

Sagan, Carl (American astronomer) 84
'show don't tell' in writing 81
similes 116
'sombunall' (some but not all) and generalisations 169
speculating 13
stream of consciousness thinking 10
summarising 148
synaesthesia (cross matching senses) 62

thinking time 33
training the neurology 43

VAK (visual, auditory, kinaesthetic use of the imagination) 42, 158
visual thinking 27

water as a metaphor for thinking 10
what-if thinking 19, 91
wordplay 38
working method in writing 48
worrying 168
would-be thinking 27
would you rather game 95

For Product Safety Concerns and Information please contact our EU
representative GPSR@taylorandfrancis.com
Taylor & Francis Verlag GmbH, Kaufingerstraße 24, 80331 München, Germany

www.ingramcontent.com/pod-product-compliance
Lightning Source LLC
Chambersburg PA
CBHW081946230426
43669CB00019B/2940